THE POWER OF YOUR SUBCONSCIOUS MIND SUBLIMINAL PROGRAM

Books by Joseph Murphy

How to Use the Laws of the Mind

Psychic Perception

Telepsychics

Maximize Your Potential Through the Power of Your Subconscious Mind to Create Wealth and Success

Maximize Your Potential Through the Power of Your Subconscious Mind to Develop Self Confidence and Self-Esteem

Maximize Your Potential Through the Power of Your Subconscious Mind for An Enriched Life

Maximize Your Potential Through the Power of Your Subconscious Mind to Overcome Fear and Worry

Maximize Your Potential Through the Power of Your Subconscious Mind for Health and Vitality

Maximize Your Potential Through the Power of Your Subconscious Mind for A More Spiritual Life

THE POWER OF YOUR SUBCONSCIOUS MIND SUBLIMINAL PROGRAM

For Relaxation and Self-Confidence,
Health and Well-Being, Wealth and
Success, and Harmonic Relations

DR. JOSEPH MURPHY

MEDIA

Published 2022 by Gildan Media LLC
aka G&D Media
www.GandDmedia.com

THE POWER OF YOUR SUBCONSCIOUS MIND SUBLIMINAL PROGRAM.
Copyright © Joseph Murphy Trust. All rights exclusively licensed by
JMW Group Inc., jmwgroup@jmwgroup.net.

Front cover design by David Rheinhardt of Pyrographx

Interior design by Meghan Day Healey of Story Horse, LLC

Library of Congress Cataloging-in-Publication Data is available upon
request

ISBN: 978-1-7225-0593-6

10 9 8 7 6 5 4 3 2 1

CONTENTS

INTRODUCTION

Is there an answer to why some people are happy and successful and others are suffering? There most certainly is.

For the express purpose of answering and clarifying this question and many others of a similar nature, I was motivated to write this book. I urge you to study this discussion and apply the techniques outlined herein. As you do, I feel absolutely convinced that you will lay hold of a miracle-working power that will lift you up from confusion, misery, melancholy, and failure, and guide you to your true place, solve your difficulties, sever you from emotional and physical bondage, and place you on the royal road to freedom, happiness, and peace of mind.

This miracle-working power of your subconscious mind can heal you of your sickness and make you vital and strong again. In learning how to use your inner powers, you will open the prison door of fear and enter into a life described by Paul as the glorious liberty of the sons of God.

This book conveys the foundations of positive thinking and will inspire you to do exercises to help make you, without exception, more successful, healthier, and happier. The four main parts will acquaint you with the basic laws of mind in crucial areas of our lives: relaxation and self-confidence, health and well-being, wealth and success, and harmonious relationships. You will find exercises in each area. I suggest you read the affirmations with calming music of your choice. This will affect your subconscious if you do this often.

You should read the meditations daily while listening to calming music so you can enter into a state of relaxation. In this state you will be able to bring about the changes you are longing for. Soon you will feel firsthand that you are the master of your life. The structure of a relaxation exercise is always the same: initiation of relaxation, deepening of relaxation, visualization, and return into your everyday consciousness.

Each chapter also contains messages that you should read and allow your subconscious to perceive, thus allowing your mind to influence their meaning. Since the messages are positive affirmations, they will change your subconscious and your life for the better. Many studies show that repeated messages can have a strong influence on us and have long been applied successfully in various forms of therapy. Of course, the strength of the effect depends on how often you let your subconscious absorb these messages. At the outset of each exercise, you should read the affirmations.

When you are busy with housekeeping, jogging, walking, exercising, or even when you're driving a car, repeat the affirmations in your mind. This will amplify their effects by a huge factor and help you to achieve everything you wish for and dream of in the respective areas of your life.

You will become acquainted with the laws of the mind. My phenomenal message is quite simple: You are what you think day by day—that is, what you think in your heart of hearts. Everything you think, believe, and feel is imprinted on your subconscious. And your subconscious will express—through your personality and the reality of your life—everything you have imprinted on it.

The conclusion is simple: You must think positively. You should feed your subconscious life-affirming and uplifting content and protect it from negative influences—your own negativity or discouragement from external sources.

Let us begin.

PART I
Relaxation and Self-Confidence

CHAPTER ONE

The Subliminal Messages

D o you feel the strength and the positive energy that courses through you when you read these sentences with awareness?

- I can change my life at any time.
- All I have to do is to change my thoughts and my beliefs.
- This will also change my feelings.
- I will always choose what is life-affirming and constructive.
- From this very moment I alone will decide what I think.
- I have decided to win in my life.
- I make the best of myself.
- I courageously accept life's challenges.
- I will make it.

- I forgive myself what I have done wrong so far.
- I also forgive all people who may have hurt me in the past.
- I forget the past. I am looking ahead.
- I wish peace, harmony, and all blessings of life on all people.
- My views and convictions are constructive.
- In this way the power of my subconscious opens every door for me.
- It is good to be alive and I am grateful for it.

The Treasure House within You

The secret of happy and successful people is their ability to communicate with their subconscious and tap its energies. You can do this as well because your inner world contains a limitless power. Look within and you will find the fulfillment of your wishes. More precise information will be provided later in this chapter.

Everything Good Is Within You

Infinite riches are all around you if you will open your mental eyes and behold the treasure house of infinity within you. There is a gold mine there from which you can extract everything you need to live life gloriously, joyously, and abundantly.

Many people are sound asleep because they do not know about this gold mine of infinite intelligence and boundless love within themselves. Whatever you want, you can draw forth. A magnetized piece of steel will lift about twelve times its own weight, and if you demagnetize this same piece of steel, it will not lift even a feather.

Similarly, there are two types of people. There is the magnetized person who is full of confidence and faith. They know that they are born to win and to succeed. Then, there is the type of person who is demagnetized. They are full of fears and doubts. Opportunities come, and they say, "I might fail; I might lose my money; people will laugh at me." This type of person will not get very far in life because, if they are afraid to go forward, they will simply stay where they are. Become a magnetized person and discover the master secret of the ages.

The Master Secret of the Ages

What, in your opinion, is the master secret of the ages? The secret of atomic energy? Thermonuclear energy? The neutron bomb? Interplanetary travel? No—not any of these. Then, what is this master secret? Where can one find it, and how can it be contacted and brought into action?

The answer is extraordinarily simple. This secret is the marvelous miracle-working power found in your own subconscious mind—the last place that most people would seek it.

Example: A woman wrote to me as follows: "I am seventy-five years old, a widow with a grown family. I was living alone and on a pension. I heard your lectures on the powers of the subconscious mind wherein you said that ideas could be conveyed to the subconscious mind by repetition, faith, and expectancy.

"I began to repeat frequently with feeling, 'I am wanted. I am happily married to a kind, loving, and spiritual-minded man. I am secure.'

"I kept on doing this many times a day for about two weeks, and one day at the corner drugstore, I was introduced to a retired pharmacist. I found him to be kind, understanding, and very religious. He was a perfect answer to my prayer. Within a week he proposed to me, and now we are on our honeymoon in Europe. I know that the intelligence within my subconscious mind brought both of us together in divine order."

The Marvelous Power of Your Subconscious

You can bring into your life more power, more wealth, more health, more happiness, and more joy by learning to contact and release the hidden power of your subconscious mind. You need not acquire this power; you already possess it. But you want to learn how to use it, and you want to understand it so that you can apply it in all departments of your life.

As you follow the simple techniques and processes set forth in this book, you can gain the necessary knowledge and understanding. You can be inspired by a new light, and you can generate a new force enabling you to realize your hopes and make all your dreams come true. Decide now to make your life grander, greater, richer, and nobler than ever before.

Within your subconscious depths lie infinite wisdom, infinite power, and infinite supply of all that is necessary, which is waiting for development and expression. Begin now to recognize these potentialities of your deeper mind, and they will take form in the world without.

The infinite intelligence within your subconscious mind can reveal to you everything you need to know at every moment of time and point of space, provided you are open-minded and receptive. You can receive new thoughts and ideas enabling you to bring forth new inventions, make new discoveries, or write books and plays. Moreover, the infinite intelligence in your subconscious can impart to you wonderful kinds of knowledge of an original nature. It can reveal to you and open the way for perfect expression and true place in your life.

Through the wisdom of your subconscious mind, you can attract the ideal companion, as well as the right business associate or partner. This wisdom can help you find the right buyer for your home and pro-vide you with all the money you need, and the finan-cial freedom to be, to do, and to have as your heart desires.

It is your right to discover this inner world of thought, feeling, and power, of light, love, and beauty. Though invisible, its forces are mighty. Within your subconscious mind you will find the solution for every problem, and the cause for every effect. Because you can draw out the hidden powers, you come into actual possession of the power and wisdom neces-sary to move forward in abundance, security, joy, and dominion.

I have seen the power of the subconscious lift people up out of crippled states, making them whole, vital, and strong once more, and free to go out into the world to experience happiness, health, and joyous expression. Your subconscious holds a miraculous healing power that can heal the troubled mind and the broken heart. It can open the prison door of the mind and liberate you. It can free you from all kinds of material and physical bondage.

Necessity of a Working Basis

Substantial progress in any field of endeavor is impos-sible in the absence of a working basis that is universal in its application. You can become skilled in the operation of your subconscious mind. You can practice its powers with a certainty of results in exact proportion to your knowledge of its principles and to your application of them for definite specific purposes and goals you wish to achieve.

Being a former chemist, I would like to point out that if you combine hydrogen and oxygen in the proportions of two atoms of the former to one of the latter, water will be the result. You are very familiar with the fact that one atom of oxygen and one atom of carbon will produce carbon monoxide, a poisonous gas. But if you add another atom of oxygen, you will get carbon dioxide, a harmless gas, and so on throughout the vast realm of chemical compounds.

You must not think that the principles of chemistry, physics, and mathematics differ from the principles of your subconscious mind. Let us consider a generally accepted principle: "Water seeks its own level." This is a universal principle that is applicable to water everywhere.

Consider another principle: "Matter expands when heated." This is true anywhere, at any time, and under all circumstances. You can heat a piece of steel, and it will expand regardless of whether the steel is found in China, England, or India. It is a universal truth that matter expands when heated. It is also a universal truth that whatever you impress on your subconscious mind is expressed on the screen of space as condition, experience, and event.

Your prayer is answered because your subconscious mind is principle, and by principle, I mean the way a thing works. For example, the principle of electricity is that it works from a higher to a lower potential. You do not change the principle of electricity when you use it, but by cooperating with nature, you can bring forth marvelous inventions and discoveries that bless humanity in countless ways.

Your subconscious mind is principle and works according to the law of belief. You must know what belief is, why it works, and how it works. Your Bible says this in a simple, clear, and beautiful way: "Whosoever shall say unto this mountain, Be thou removed, and be thou cast into the sea; and shall not doubt in his heart, but shall believe that those things which he saith shall come to pass; he shall have whatsoever he saith." Mark 11:23

The law of your mind is the law of belief. This means to believe in the way your mind works, to believe in belief itself. The belief of your mind is the thought of your mind—that is simple—just that and nothing else.

All your experiences, events, conditions, and acts are the reactions of your subconscious mind to your thoughts. Remember, it is not the thing believed in, but the belief in your own mind that brings about the result. Cease believing in the false beliefs, opinions, superstitions, and fears of humankind. Begin to believe in the eternal verities and truths of life, which never change. Then, you will move onward, upward, and Godward.

Whoever reads this book and applies the principles of the subconscious mind herein set forth will be able to pray scientifically and effectively for themselves and for others. Your prayer is answered according to the universal law of action and reaction. Thought is incipient action. The reaction is the response from your subconscious mind, which corresponds with the nature of your thought. Busy your mind with the concepts of harmony, health, peace, and goodwill, and wonders will happen in your life.

Example: A young girl, a student at the University of Southern California, said to me, "I didn't have the money to buy that bag, but now I know where to find money and all the things I need, and that is in the treasure house of eternity within me."

The Conscious and Subconscious Minds

An excellent way to get acquainted with the two functions of your mind is to look upon your own mind as a garden. You are a gardener, and you are planting seeds (thoughts) in your subconscious mind all day long, based on your habitual thinking. As you sow in your subconscious mind, so shall you reap in your body and environment.

Begin now to sow thoughts of peace, happiness, right action, goodwill, and prosperity. Think quietly and with interest on these qualities and accept them fully in your conscious reasoning mind. Continue to plant these wonderful seeds (thoughts) in the garden of your mind, and you will reap a glorious harvest. Your subconscious mind may be likened to the soil that will grow all kinds of seeds, good or bad. Do men gather grapes of thorns, or figs of thistles? Every thought is, therefore, a cause, and every condition is an effect. For this reason, it is essential that you take charge of your thoughts so as to bring forth only desirable conditions.

When your mind thinks correctly, when you understand the truth, when the thoughts deposited in your subconscious mind are constructive, harmonious, and peaceful, the magic working power of your subconscious will respond and bring about harmonious conditions, agreeable surroundings, and the best of everything. When you begin to control your thought processes, you can apply the powers of your subconscious to any problem or difficulty. In other words, you will actually be consciously cooperating with the infinite power and omnipotent law that governs all things.

Look around you wherever you live and you will notice that the vast majority of humanity live in the world without; the more enlightened among us are intensely interested in the world within. Remember, it is the world within—namely, your thoughts, feelings, and imagery—that makes your world without. It is, therefore, the only creative power, and everything you find in your world of expression has been created by you in the inner world of your mind, consciously or unconsciously.

A knowledge of the interaction of your conscious and subconscious minds will enable you to transform your whole life. In order to change external conditions, you must change the cause. Most people try to change conditions and circumstances by working with conditions and circumstances. To remove discord, confusion, lack, and limitation, however, you must remove the cause, and the cause is the way you are using your conscious mind. In other words, the way you are thinking and picturing in your mind.

Example: One time Caruso, the great operatic tenor, was struck with stage fright. He said his throat was paralyzed due to spasms caused by intense fear, which constricted the muscles of his throat. Perspiration poured copiously down his face. He was ashamed because he had to go out on the stage, yet he was shaking with fear and trepidation.

He said, "They will laugh at me. I can't sing." Then he shouted in the presence of those behind the stage, "The Little Me wants to strangle the Big Me within."

He said to the Little Me, "Get out of here, the Big Me wants to sing through me."

By the Big Me, he meant the limitless power and wisdom of his subconscious mind, and he began to shout, "Get out, get out, the Big Me is going to sing."

His subconscious mind responded by releasing the vital forces within him. When the call came, he walked out on the stage and sang gloriously and majestically, enthralling the audience.

Every Thought Counts—and Works

To remove discord, confusion, lack, and limitation, you must remove the cause, and the cause is the way you are using your conscious mind—in other words, the way you are thinking and picturing in your mind.

You are living in a fathomless sea of infinite riches. Your subconscious is very sensitive to your thoughts. Your thoughts form the mold or matrix through which the infinite intelligence, wisdom, vital forces, and energies of your subconscious flow. The practical application of the laws of your mind as illustrated in each chapter of this book will cause you to experience abundance for poverty, wisdom for superstition and ignorance, peace for pain, joy for sadness, light for darkness, harmony for discord, faith and confidence for fear, success for failure, and freedom from the law of averages. Certainly, there can be no more wonderful blessing than these from a mental, emotional, and material standpoint.

Most of the great scientists, artists, poets, singers, writers, and inventors have a deep understanding of the workings of the conscious and subconscious minds.

Outstanding Differences and Modes of Operation

You will perceive the main differences by the following illustrations: The conscious mind is like the navigator or captain at the bridge of a ship. The captain directs the ship and signals orders to the crew in the engine room, who in turn control all the boilers, instruments, gauges, and so on. The workers in the engine room do not know where they are going; they follow orders. They would go on the rocks if the captain on the bridge issued faulty or wrong instructions based on the findings with the compass, sextant, or other instruments. The workers in the engine room obey the captain because the captain is in charge and issues orders, which are automatically obeyed. Members of the crew do not talk back to the captain; they simply carry out orders.

The captain is the master of the ship, and his or her decrees are carried out. Likewise, your conscious mind is the captain and the master of your ship, which represents your body, environment, and all your affairs. Your subconscious mind takes the orders you give it based upon what your conscious mind believes and accepts as true.

When you repeatedly say to people, "I can't afford it," then your subconscious mind takes you at your word and sees to it that you will not be in a position to purchase what you want. As long as you persist in saying, "I can't afford that car, that trip to Europe, that home, that fur coat or ermine wrap," you can rest assured that your subconscious mind will follow your orders, and you will go through life experiencing the lack of all these things.

Another simple illustration is this: When you say, "I do not like mushrooms," and the occasion subsequently comes that you are served mushrooms in sauces or salads, you will get indigestion because your subconscious mind says to you, "The boss (your conscious mind) does not like mushrooms." This is an amusing example of the outstanding differences and modes of operation of your conscious and subconscious minds.

A woman may say, "I wake up at three o'clock, if I drink coffee at night." Whenever she drinks coffee, her subconscious mind nudges her, as if to say, "The boss wants you to stay awake tonight."

Your subconscious mind works twenty-four hours a day and makes provisions for your benefit, pouring all the fruit of your habitual thinking into your lap.

You Are the Boss

Your situation is similar to that of the ship's captain at the rudder of the ship. The captain has to give the correct commands. And you have to give the right commands to your subconscious, which influences your whole life in the form of thoughts and imaginings. Change your habits of thought and you will influence fate itself.

Exercise: Three Steps to Your Goal

The following method will infallibly lead to success:

1. Look at your problem from all angles.
2. Instruct your subconscious to find the best solution.
3. Indulge in the firm conviction that your request will be settled as quickly as possible.

CHAPTER TWO

How Your Own Mind Works

In this chapter, I will discuss how you can orient your thinking to the principles and maxims of life and how not to let yourself be deceived by fear, ignorance, and superstition. Don't let anyone dictate your thoughts. Think and decide for yourself. Whatever your subconscious deems as right and is convinced of, it will accept as the truth and try to put into practice. So you should believe in your luck, in your intuition, in the validity of your decisions, and in all the wonderful things in life.

Your Subconsciousness Is Very Active

You have a mind, and you should learn how to use it. There are two levels of your mind—the conscious or rational level, and the subconscious or irrational level.

You think with your conscious mind, and whatever you habitually think sinks down into your subconscious mind, which creates according to the nature of your thoughts. Your subconscious mind is the seat of your emotions and is the creative mind. If you think good thoughts, then good will follow; if you think evil, evil will follow. This is the way your mind works.

The main point to remember is once the subconscious mind accepts an idea, it begins to execute it. It is an interesting and subtle truth that the law of the subconscious mind works for good and bad ideas alike. This law, when applied in a negative way, is the cause of failure, frustration, and unhappiness. However, when your habitual thinking is harmonious and constructive, you experience perfect health, success, and prosperity.

Peace of mind and a healthy body are inevitable when you begin to think and feel in the right way. Whatever you claim mentally and feel as true, your subconscious mind will accept and bring forth into your experience. The only act necessary for you to do is to get your subconscious mind to accept your idea, and the law of your own subconscious mind will bring forth the health, peace, or the position you desire. You give the command or decree, and your subconscious will faithfully reproduce the idea impressed upon it. The law of your mind is this: you will get a reaction or response from your subconscious mind according to the nature of the thought or idea you hold in your conscious mind.

Psychologists and psychiatrists point out that when thoughts are conveyed to your subconscious mind, impressions are made in the brain cells. As soon as your subconscious accepts any idea, your mind proceeds to put it into effect immediately. The process works by association of ideas and uses every bit of knowledge that you have gathered in your lifetime to bring about its purpose. You draw on the infinite power, energy, and wisdom within you, which lines up all the laws of nature to get its way. Sometimes it seems to bring about an immediate solution to your difficulties, but at other times your idea may take days, weeks, or longer to process. Its ways are past finding out.

Example: A seventy-five-year-old woman was in the habit of saying to herself, "I am losing my memory." She reversed the procedure and practiced induced autosuggestion several times a day by thinking consciously: "My memory from today on is improving in every department. I shall always remember whatever I need to know at every moment of time and point of space. The impressions received will be clearer and more definite. I shall retain them automatically and with ease. Whatever I wish to recall will immediately present itself in the correct form in my mind. I am improving rapidly every day, and very soon my memory will be better than it has ever been before." At the end of three weeks, her memory was back to normal, and she was delighted.

Conscious and *Subconscious* Terms Differentiated

You must remember that these are not two minds. They are merely two spheres of activity within one mind. Your conscious mind is the reasoning mind. It is that phase of mind that chooses. For example, you choose your books, your home, and your partner in life. You make all your decisions with your conscious mind.

On the other hand, without any conscious choice on your part, your heart is kept functioning automatically, and the process of digestion, circulation, and breathing are carried on by your subconscious mind through processes independent of your conscious control.

Your subconscious mind accepts what is impressed upon it or what you consciously believe. It does not reason things out like your conscious mind, and it does not argue with you controversially. Your subconscious mind is like the soil that accepts any kind of seed, good or bad. Your thoughts are active and might be likened as seeds. Negative, destructive thoughts continue to work negatively in your subconscious mind, and in due time will come forth into outer experience that corresponds with them.

Remember, your subconscious mind does not engage in proving whether your thoughts are good or bad, true or false, but it responds according to the nature of your thoughts or suggestions. For example, if you consciously assume something as true, even though it may be false, your subconscious mind will accept it as true and proceed to bring about results that must necessarily follow, because you consciously assumed it to be true.

The Terms *Objective* and *Subjective* Mind Clarified

Your conscious mind is sometimes referred to as your objective mind because it deals with outward objects. The objective mind takes cognizance of the objective world. Its media of observation are your five physical senses. Your objective mind is your guide and director in contact with your environment. You gain knowledge through your five senses. Your objective mind learns through observation, experience, and education. As previously pointed out, the greatest function of the objective mind is that of reasoning.

Suppose you are one of the thousands of tourists who come to Los Angeles annually. You would conclude that it is a beautiful city based upon your observation of the parks, pretty gardens, majestic buildings, and lovely homes. This is the working of your objective mind.

Your subconscious mind is often referred to as your subjective mind. Your subjective mind takes cognizance of its environment by means independent of the five senses. Your subjective mind perceives by intuition. It is the seat of your emotion and the storehouse of memory. Your subjective mind performs its highest functions when your objective senses are in abeyance. In a word, it is intelligence that makes itself manifest when the objective mind is suspended or in a sleepy, drowsy state.

Your subjective mind sees without the use of the natural organs of vision. It has the capacity of clairvoyance and clairaudience. Your subjective mind can leave your body, travel to distant lands, and bring back information often of the most exact and truthful character. Through your subjective mind you can read the thoughts of others, read the contents of sealed envelopes and closed safes. Your subjective mind has the ability to apprehend the thoughts of others without the use of the ordinary objective means of communication. It is of the greatest importance that we understand the interaction of the objective and subjective mind in order to learn the true art of prayer.

The Subconscious Cannot Reason
Like Your Conscious Mind

Your subconscious mind cannot argue controversially. Hence, if you give it wrong suggestions, it will accept them as true and will proceed to bring them to pass as conditions, experiences, and events. All things that have happened to you are based on thoughts impressed on your subconscious mind through belief.

If you have conveyed erroneous concepts to your subconscious mind, the sure method of overcoming them is by the repetition of constructive, harmonious thoughts frequently repeated, which your subconscious mind accepts, thus forming new and healthy habits of thought and life, for your subconscious mind is the seat of habit.

The habitual thinking of your conscious mind establishes deep grooves in your subconscious mind. This is favorable for you if your habitual thoughts are harmonious, peaceful, and constructive. But if you have indulged in fear, worry, and other destructive forms of thinking, the remedy is to recognize the omnipotence of your subconscious mind and decree freedom, happiness, and perfect health. Your subconscious mind, being creative and one with your divine source, will proceed to create the freedom and happiness you have earnestly decreed.

Example: Dr. Evelyn Fleet, a colleague of mine, told me about an article in the English newspapers dealing with the power of suggestion. This is the suggestion a man gave to his subconscious mind over a period of about two years: "I would give my right arm to see my daughter cured."

It seems his daughter had a crippling form of arthritis together with a so-called incurable form of skin disease. Medical treatment had failed to alleviate the condition, and the father had an intense longing for his daughter's healing, and he expressed his desire in the words just quoted.

The newspaper article pointed out that one day the family was out driving when their car collided with another. The father's right arm was torn off at the shoulder, and immediately the daughter's arthritis and skin condition vanished.

You must make certain to give your subconscious only suggestions that heal, bless, elevate, and inspire you in all ways. Remember that your subconscious mind cannot take a joke. It takes you at your word.

The Tremendous Power of Suggestion

You must realize by now that your conscious mind is the "watchman at the gate," and its chief function is to protect your subconscious mind from false impressions. You are now aware of one of the basic laws of the mind: your subconscious mind is amenable to suggestion.

As you know, your subconscious mind does not make comparisons, or contrasts; neither does it reason or think things out for itself. This latter function belongs to your conscious mind. It simply reacts to the impressions given to it by your conscious mind. It does not show a preference for one course of action over another.

Here is a classic example of the tremendous power of suggestion. Suppose you approach a timid-looking passenger on board ship and say to him something like this: "You look very ill. How pale you are. I feel certain you are going to be seasick. Let me help you to your cabin."

The passenger turns pale. Your suggestion of seasickness associates itself with his own fears and forebodings. He accepts your aid down to the berth, and there your negative suggestion, which was accepted by him, is realized.

It is true that different people will react in different ways to the same suggestion because of their subconscious conditioning or belief. For example, if you go to a sailor on the ship and say to him sympathetically, "My dear fellow, you're looking very ill. Are you feeling sick? You look to me as if you are going to be seasick."

According to his temperament he either laughs at your joke or expresses a mild irritation. Your suggestion fell on deaf ears in this instance because your suggestion of seasickness was associated in his mind with his own immunity from it. Therefore, it called up not fear or worry, but self-confidence.

How Autosuggestion Banishes Fear

Autosuggestion means suggesting something definite and specific to oneself. Herbert Parkyn, in his excellent manual on autosuggestion, records the following amusing incident: A New York visitor in Chicago looks at his watch, which is set an hour ahead of Chicago time, and tells a Chicago friend that it is twelve o'clock. The Chicago friend, not considering the difference in time between Chicago and New York, tells the New Yorker that he is hungry and that he must go to lunch.

Autosuggestion may be used to banish various fears and other negative conditions. A young singer was invited to give an audition. She had been looking forward to the interview, but on three previous occasions she had failed miserably due to fear of failure. This young lady had a lovely voice, but she had been saying to herself, "When the time comes for me to sing, maybe they won't like me. I will try, but I'm full of fear and anxiety."

Her subconscious mind accepted these negative autosuggestions as a request and proceeded to manifest them and bring them into her experience. The cause was an involuntary autosuggestion—that is, silent fear thoughts emotionalized and subjectified.

She overcame her fear with the following technique: Three times a day she isolated herself in a room. She sat down comfortably in an armchair, relaxed her body, and closed her eyes. She stilled her mind and body as best she could. Physical inertia favors mental passivity and renders the mind more receptive to suggestion.

She counteracted the fear suggestion by saying to herself, "I sing beautifully. I am poised, serene, confident, and calm." She repeated this statement slowly, quietly, and with feeling from five to ten times at each sitting. She had three such sittings every day and one immediately prior to going to sleep. At the end of a week she was completely poised and confident. When the invitation to audition came, she gave a remarkable, wonderful audition.

How to Overcome a Nasty Temper

Many who complained of irritability and bad temper proved to be very susceptible to autosuggestion and obtained marvelous results by using the following statements three or four times a day—morning, noon, and at night prior to sleep for about a month: "Henceforth, I shall grow more good-humored. Joy, happiness, and cheerfulness are now becoming my normal states of mind. Every day I am becoming more and more lovable and understanding. I am now becoming the center of cheer and goodwill to all those about me, infecting them with good humor. This happy, joyous, and cheerful mood is now becoming my normal, natural state of mind. I am grateful."

The Constructive and Destructive Power of Suggestion

Some illustrations and comments on heterosuggestion: heterosuggestion means suggestions from another person. In all ages the power of suggestion has played a part in the life and thought of humans in every period of time and in each country of the earth. In many parts of the world it is the controlling power in religion.

Suggestion may be used to discipline and control ourselves, but it can also be used to take control and command over others who do not know the laws of mind. In its constructive form it is wonderful and magnificent. In its negative aspects it is one of the most destructive of all the response patterns of the mind, resulting in patterns of misery, failure, suffering, sickness, and disaster.

Have You Accepted Any of These?

From infancy on, most of us have been given many negative suggestions. Not knowing how to thwart them, we unconsciously accepted them. Here are some of the negative suggestions: "You can't." "You'll never amount to anything." "You mustn't." "You'll fail." "You haven't got a chance." "You're all wrong." "It's no use." "It's not what you know, but who you know." "The world is going to the dogs." "What's the use, nobody cares." "It's no use trying so hard." "You're too old now." "Things are getting worse and worse." "Life is an endless grind." "Love is for the birds." "You just can't win." "Pretty soon you'll be bankrupt." "Watch out, you'll get the virus." "You can't trust a soul," and so on.

Unless, as an adult, you use constructive auto-suggestion, which is a reconditioning therapy, the impressions made on you in the past can cause behavior patterns that cause failure in your personal and social life. Autosuggestion is a means releasing you from the mass of negative verbal conditioning that might otherwise distort your life pattern, making the development of good habits difficult.

Example: A college professor said to me, "Everything in my life is topsy-turvy, and I have lost health, wealth, and friends. Everything I touch turns out wrong."

I explained to him that he should establish a major premise in his thinking, that the infinite intelligence of his subconscious mind was guiding, directing, and prospering him spiritually, mentally, and materially. Then, his subconscious mind would automatically direct him wisely in his investments, decisions, and also heal his body and restore his mind to peace and tranquility.

This professor formulated an overall picture of the way he wanted his life to be, and this was his major premise: "Infinite intelligence leads and guides me in all my ways. Perfect health is mine, and the law of harmony operates in my mind and body. Beauty, love, peace, and abundance are mine. The principle of right action and divine order govern my entire life. I know my major premise is based on the eternal truths of life, and I know, feel, and believe that my subconscious mind responds according to the nature of my conscious mind thinking."

Later he wrote me as follows: "I repeated the statements slowly, quietly, and lovingly several times a day knowing that they were sinking deep down into my subconscious mind, and that results must follow. I am deeply grateful for the interview you gave me, and I would like to add that all departments of my life are changing for the better. It works."

The Subconscious Does Not Argue Controversially

Your subconscious mind is all wise and knows the answers to all questions. It does not argue with you or talk back to you. It does not say, "You must not impress me with that." For example, when you say, "I am too old now" or "I can't meet this obligation," you are impregnating your subconscious to do this. If you say, "I was born on the wrong side," with these negative thoughts, your subconscious mind responds accordingly. You are actually blocking your own good, thereby bringing lack, limitation, and frustration into your life.

When you set up obstacles, impediments, and delays in your conscious mind, you are denying the wisdom and intelligence resident in your subconscious mind. You are actually saying in effect that your subconscious mind cannot solve your problem. This leads to mental and emotional congestion, followed by sickness and neurotic tendencies.

To realize your desire to overcome your frustration, affirm boldly several times a day: "The infinite intelligence that gave me this desire leads, guides, and reveals to me the perfect plan for the unfolding of my desire. I know the deeper wisdom of my subconscious is now responding, and what I feel and claim within is expressed in the without. There is a balance, equilibrium, and equanimity."

If you say, "There is no way out; I am lost; there is no way out of this dilemma; I am stymied and blocked," you will get no answer or response from your subconscious mind. If you want the subconscious to work for you, give it the right request, and attain its cooperation. It is always working for you. It is controlling your heartbeat this minute and also your breathing. It heals a cut on your finger, and its tendency is lifeward, forever seeking to take care of you and preserve you. Your subconscious has a mind of its own, but it accepts your patterns of thought and imagery.

When you are seeking an answer to a problem, your subconscious will respond, but it expects you to come to a decision and to a true judgment in your conscious mind. You must acknowledge the answer is in your subconscious mind. However, if you say, "I don't think there is any way out; I am all mixed up and confused; why don't I get an answer?" you are neutralizing your prayer. Like the soldier marking time, you do not get anywhere.

Still the wheels of your mind, relax, let go, and quietly affirm: "My subconscious knows the answer. It is responding to me now. I give thanks because I know the infinite intelligence of my subconscious knows all things and is revealing the perfect answer to me now. My real conviction is now setting free the majesty and glory of my subconscious mind. I rejoice that it is so."

You are the boss of your soul, of your subconscious and your fate. Always remember: You have the choice. Choose life. Choose love. Choose health. Choose good fortune.

Exercise: Protection Against Negative Suggestions

One glance at a newspaper is enough to arouse sorrow, fear, and doubt in every person who is only marginally sensitive. A person who does nothing to oppose such negative thoughts endangers their will to live. For this very reason it is calming to know that positive auto-suggestions are an effective form of protection against all forms of negative influences.

So thoroughly check every now and then if and how your surroundings try to influence you in a negative way. You are by no means helpless against suggestions from without. In the past years and decades you have probably suffered enough from this. Just think of the many derogatory remarks your family, your friends, and relatives but especially teachers, trainers, and colleagues have made. A critical examination will show you that a lot of it has been completely beside the point and has only been said to upset or suppress you.

Now it is time to become aware of these subtle mechanisms, to repudiate them and oppose them with positive thoughts and statements.

CHAPTER THREE

Live Relaxed and Self-Confident

Each problem has its own solution within itself. Each question contains an answer. Infinite wisdom will aid those who call upon it with trust. This chapter may surprise you with its fresh perspective about habits, the overcoming of fear, and the age of the dawning wisdom.

How Your Subconscious Removes Mental Blocks

If you are presented with a difficult situation and you cannot see your way clear, the best procedure is to assume that infinite intelligence within your subconscious mind knows all and sees all, has the answer, and is revealing it to you now. Your new mental attitude that the creative intelligence is bringing about a happy solution will enable you to find the answer.

Rest assured that such an attitude of mind will bring order, peace, and meaning to all your undertakings.

How to Break or Build a Habit

You are a creature of habit. Habit is the function of your subconscious mind. You learned to swim, ride a bicycle, dance, and drive a car by consciously doing these activities over and over until they established tracks in your subconscious mind. Then, the automatic habit action of your subconscious mind took over. This is sometimes called second nature, which is a reaction of your subconscious mind to your thinking and acting.

You are free to choose a good habit or a bad habit. If you repeat a negative thought or act over a period of time, you will be under the compulsion of a habit. The law of your subconscious is compulsion.

Example: Mr. Block, a salesman, said that he had been making an admirable annual income, but for the past three months all doors seemed to be slamming shut. He brought clients up to the point where they were about to sign on the dotted line, and then at the eleventh hour the door closed. He added that perhaps he had been jinxed.

In discussing the matter with Mr. Block, I discovered that three months previously he had become very irritated, annoyed, and resentful toward a dentist who, after he had promised to sign a contract, had withdrawn at the last moment. He began to live in the unconscious fear that other clients would do the same, thereby setting up a history of frustration, hostility, and obstacles. He gradually built up in his mind a belief in obstruction and last-minute cancellations until a vicious cycle had been established.

"What I fear most has come upon me," he said. Mr. Block realized that the trouble was in his own mind and that it was essential to change his mental attitude.

He broke his run of so-called misfortune in the following way: "I realized I am one with the infinite intelligence of my subconscious mind, which knows no obstacle, difficulty, or delay. I live in the joyous expectancy of the best. My deeper mind responds to my thoughts. I know that the work of the infinite power of my subconscious cannot be hindered. Infinite intelligence always finishes successfully whatever it begins. Creative wisdom works through me bringing all my plans and purposes to completion. Whatever I start, I bring to a successful conclusion. My aim in life is to give wonderful service, and all those whom I contact are blessed by what I have to offer. All my work comes to full fruition in divine order."

He repeated this prayer every morning before going to call on his customers, and he also prayed each night prior to sleep. In a short time he had established a new habit pattern in his subconscious mind, and he was back in his stride as a successful salesman.

How Much Do You Want What You Want?

A young man asked Socrates how he could get wisdom. Socrates replied, "Come with me." He took the lad to a river, pushed the boy's head under the water, held it there until the boy was gasping for air, then relaxed and released his head. When the boy regained his composure, he asked him, "What did you desire most when you were under water?"

"I wanted air," said the boy.

Socrates said to him, "When you want wisdom as much as you wanted air when you were immersed in the water, you will receive it."

Likewise, when you really have an intense desire to overcome any block in your life, and you come to a clear-cut decision that there is a way out, and that is the course you wish to follow, then victory and triumph are assured.

If you really want peace of mind and inner calm, you will get it. Regardless of how unjustly you have been treated, or how unfair the boss has been, or what a mean scoundrel someone has proved to be, all this makes no difference to you when you awaken to your mental and spiritual powers. You know what you want, and you will definitely refuse to let the thieves (thoughts) of hatred, anger, hostility, and ill will rob you of peace, harmony, health, and happiness.

You cease to become upset by people, conditions, news, and events by identifying your thoughts immediately with your aim in life. Your aim is peace, health, inspiration, harmony, and abundance. Feel a river of peace flowing through you now. Your thought is the immaterial and invisible power, and you choose to let it bless, inspire, and give you peace.

Why Alcohol Cannot Heal

This is a case history of a married man with four children who was supporting and secretly living with another woman during his business trips. He was ill, nervous, irritable, and cantankerous, and he could not sleep without drugs. The doctor's medicine failed to bring down his high blood pressure. He had pain in numerous organs of his body, which doctors could not diagnose or relieve. To make matters worse, he was drinking heavily.

The cause of all this was a deep unconscious sense of guilt. He had violated the marriage vows, and this troubled him. The religious creed he was brought up on was deeply lodged in his subconscious mind, and he drank excessively to heal the wound of guilt.

He listened to the explanation of how his mind worked. He faced his problem, looked at it, and gave up his dual role. He knew that his drinking was an unconscious attempt to escape. The hidden cause lodged in his subconscious mind had to be eradicated; then the healing would follow.

He began to impress his subconscious mind three or four times a day by using the following prayer: "My mind is full of peace, poise, balance, and equilibrium. The infinite lies stretched in smiling repose within me. I am not afraid of anything in the past, the present, or the future. The infinite intelligence of my subconscious mind leads, guides, and directs me in all ways. I now meet every situation with faith, poise, calmness, and confidence. I am now completely free from the habit. My mind is full of inner peace, freedom, and joy. I forgive myself; then I am forgiven. Peace, sobriety, and confidence reign supreme in my mind."

He repeated this prayer frequently, being fully aware of what he was doing and why he was doing it. Knowing what he was doing gave him the necessary faith and confidence.

I explained to him that as he spoke these statements out loud, slowly, lovingly, and meaningfully, they would gradually sink down into his subconscious mind. Like seeds, they would grow after their kind. These truths, on which he concentrated, went in through his eyes; his ears heard the sound; and the healing vibrations of these words reached his subconscious mind and obliterated all the negative mental patterns that caused all the trouble. Light dispels darkness. The constructive thought destroys the negative thought. He became a transformed man within a month.

Our Greatest Enemy

It is said that fear is our greatest enemy. Fear is behind failure, sickness, and poor human relations. Millions of people are afraid of the past, the future, old age, insanity, and death. Fear is a thought in your mind, and you are afraid of your own thoughts.

A little boy can be paralyzed with fear when he is told there is a boogeyman under his bed who is going to take him away. When his father turns on the light and shows him there is no boogeyman, the child is freed from fear. The fear in the mind of the boy was as real as if there really was a boogeyman there. He was healed of a false thought in his mind. The thing he feared did not exist.

Likewise, most of your fears have no reality. They are merely a conglomeration of sinister shadows, and shadows have no reality.

How to Use Your Subconscious Mind to Remove Fear

One of our students told me that he was invited to speak at a banquet. He said he was panic-stricken at the thought of speaking before a thousand people. He overcame his fear this way: For several nights he sat down in an armchair for about five minutes and said to himself slowly, quietly, and positively, "I am going to master this fear. I am overcoming it now. I speak with poise and confidence. I am relaxed and at ease." He acknowledged a definite law of mind and overcame his fear.

The subconscious mind is amenable to suggestion and is controlled by suggestion. When you still your mind and relax, the thoughts of your conscious mind sink down into the subconscious through a process similar to osmosis, whereby fluids separated by a porous membrane intermingle. As these positive seeds, or thoughts, sink into the subconscious area, they grow after their kind, and you become poised, serene, and calm.

Do What You Fear

Ralph Waldo Emerson, philosopher and poet, said, "Do the thing you are afraid to do, and the death of fear is certain." There was a time when I was filled with unutterable fear when standing before an audience The way I overcame it was to stand before the audience, do the thing I was afraid to do, and the death of fear was certain.

When you affirm positively that you are going to master your fears, and you come to a definite decision in your conscious mind, you release the power of the subconscious, which flows in response to the nature of your thought.

Example: I had an experience when I was about ten years of age. I accidentally fell into a pool and went down three times. I can still remember the dark water engulfing my head, and my gasping for air until another boy pulled me out at the last moment. This experience sank into my subconscious mind, and for years I feared the water.

An elderly psychologist said to me, "Go down to the swimming pool, look at the water, and say out loud in strong tones, 'I am going to master you. I can dominate you.' Then go into the water, take lessons, and overcome it."

This I did, and I mastered the water. Do not permit water to master you. Remember, you are the master of the water. When I assumed a new attitude of mind, the omnipotent power of the subconscious responded, giving me strength, faith, and confidence, and enabling me to overcome my fear.

He Blessed the Elevator

I knew an executive of a large corporation who was terrified to ride in an elevator. He would walk up five flights of stairs to his office every morning. He said that he began to bless the elevator every night and several times a day. He finally overcame his fear.

This was how he blessed the elevator: "The elevator in our building is a wonderful idea. It came out of the universal mind. It is a boon and a blessing to all our employees. It gives wonderful service. It operates in divine order. I ride in it in peace and joy. I remain silent now while the currents of life, love, and understanding flow through the patterns of my thought. In my imagination I am now in the elevator, and I step out into my office. The elevator is full of our employees. I talk to them, and they are friendly, joyous, and free. It is a wonderful experience of freedom, faith, and confidence. I give thanks."

He continued this prayer for about ten days, and on the eleventh day, he walked into the elevator with other members of the organization and felt completely free.

Examine Your Fears

The president of a large organization told me that when he was a salesman he used to walk around the block five or six times before he called on a customer. The sales manager came along one day and said to him, "Don't be afraid of the boogeyman behind the door. There is no boogeyman. It is a false belief."

The manager told him that whenever he looked at his own fears, he stared them in the face and stood up to them, looking them straight in the eye. Then they faded and shrank into insignificance.

Another Fear: Aging

Your subconscious mind never grows old. It is timeless, ageless, and endless. It is a part of the universal mind of God that was never born, and it will never die. Fatigue or old age cannot be predicated on any spiritual quality or power. Patience, kindness, veracity, humility, goodwill, peace, harmony, and brotherly love are attributes and qualities that never grow old. If you continue to generate these qualities here on this plane of life, you will always remain young in spirit.

I remember reading an article in one of our magazines some years ago that stated that a group of eminent medical doctors at the DeCourcy Clinic, in Cincinnati, Ohio, reported that age alone is not responsible for bringing about degenerative disorders. These same physicians stated that it is the fear of time, not time itself, that has a harmful aging effect on our minds and bodies, and that the neurotic fear of the effects of time may well be the cause of premature aging.

During the many years of my public life, I have had occasion to study the biographies of the famous men and women who have continued their productive activities into the years well beyond the normal span of life. Some of them achieve their greatness in old age. At the same time, it has been my privilege to meet and to know countless individuals of no prominence who, in their lesser sphere, belonged to those hardy mortals who have proved that old age of itself does not destroy the creative powers of the mind and body.

Example: A few years ago I called on an old friend in London, England. He was over eighty years of age, very ill, and obviously was yielding to his advancing years. Our conversation revealed his physical weakness, his sense of frustration, and a general deterioration almost approaching lifelessness. His cry was that he was useless and that no one wanted him. With an expression of hopelessness, he betrayed his false philosophy, "We are born, grow up, become old, good for nothing, and that's the end."

This mental attitude of futility and worthlessness was the chief reason for his sickness. He was looking forward only to senescence, and after that—nothing. Indeed, he had grown old in his thought life, and his subconscious mind brought about all the evidence of his habitual thinking.

Age Is the Dawn of Wisdom

Unfortunately, many people have the same attitude as this unhappy man. They are afraid of what they term "old age," the end, and extinction, which really means that they are afraid of life. Yet, life is endless. Age is not the flight of years, but the dawn of wisdom.

Wisdom is an awareness of the tremendous spiritual powers in your subconscious mind and the knowledge of how to apply these powers to lead a full and happy life. Get it out of your head once and for all that sixty-five, seventy-five, or eighty-five years of age is synonymous with the end for you or anybody else. It can be the beginning of a glorious, fruitful, active, and most productive life pattern, better than you have ever experienced. Believe this, expect it, and your subconscious will bring it to pass.

Welcome the Change

Old age is not a tragic occurrence. What we call the aging process is really change. It is to be welcomed joyfully and gladly as each phase of human life is a step forward on the path that has no end. Humankind has powers that transcend bodily powers. Our senses transcend our five physical senses. Our life is spiritual and eternal. We need never grow old for life, or God, cannot grow old. The Bible says that God is life. Life is self-renewing, eternal, indestructible, and the reality of all men.

The person who thinks or believes that the earthly cycle of birth, adolescence, youth, maturity, and old age is all there is to life, is indeed to be pitied. Such a person has no anchor, no hope, no vision, and no meaning in life.

This type of belief brings frustration, stagnation, cynicism, and a sense of hopelessness resulting in neurosis and mental aberrations of all kinds. If you cannot play a fast game of tennis, or swim as fast as your child, or if your body has slowed down, or you walk with a slow step, remember life is always clothing itself anew. What we call death is but a journey to a new city in another dimension of life.

You Are as Young as You Think You Are

I gave public lectures in Caxton Hall, London, England, every few years, and following one of these lectures, a surgeon said to me, "I am eighty-four years of age. I operate every morning, visit patients in the afternoons, and I write for medical and other scientific journals in the evening."

His attitude was that he was as useful as he believed himself to be, and that he was as young as his thoughts. He said to me, "It's true what you said, 'Man is as strong as he thinks he is, and as valuable as he thinks he is.'"

This surgeon has not surrendered to advancing years. He knows that he is immortal. His final comment to me was, "If I should pass on tomorrow, I would be operating on people in the next dimension, not with a surgeon's scalpel, but with mental and spiritual surgery."

Your Gray Hair Is an Asset

Don't ever quit a job and say, "I am retired, I am old, I am finished." That would be stagnation, death, and you would be finished. Some of us are old at thirty, while others are young at eighty. The mind is the master weaver, the architect, the designer, and the sculptor. George Bernard Shaw was active at ninety, and the artistic quality of his mind had not relaxed from active duty.

I meet men and women who tell me that some employers almost slam the door in their faces when they say they are over forty. This attitude on the part of the employers is to be considered cold, callous, evil, and completely void of compassion and understanding. The total emphasis seems to be on youth—that is, you must be under thirty-five to receive consideration.

The reasoning behind this is certainly very shallow. If the employer would stop and think, they would realize that the man or woman was not selling their age or gray hair, rather, they were willing to give of their talents, their experience, and their wisdom gathered through years of experience in the marketplace of life.

Your age should be a distinct asset to any organization, because of your practice and application through the years of the principles of the Golden Rule and the law of love and goodwill. Your gray hair, if you have any, should stand for greater wisdom, skill, and understanding. Your emotional and spiritual maturity should be a tremendous blessing to any organization.

Employees should not be asked to resign when they are sixty-five. That is the time of life when they could be most useful in handling personnel problems, planning for the future, making decisions, and guiding others in the realm of creative ideas based on their experience and insight into the nature of the business.

Fear of Old Age

Many people fear old age and are uncertain about their future because they anticipate mental and physical deterioration as the years advance. What they think and feel comes to pass.

You grow old when you lose interest in life, when you cease to dream, don't hunger after new truths, and fail to search for new worlds to conquer. When your mind is open to new ideas, new interests, and when you raise the curtain and let in the sunshine and inspiration of new truths of life and the universe, you will be young and vital.

If you are sixty-five or ninety-five years of age, realize you have much to give. You can help stabilize, advise, and direct the younger generation. You can give the benefit of your knowledge, your experience, and your wisdom. You can always look ahead, for at all times you are gazing into infinite life. You will find that you can never cease to unveil the glories and wonders of life. Try to learn something new every moment of the day, and you will find your mind will always be young.

Example: Some years ago while lecturing in Bombay, India, I was introduced to a man who said he was 110 years old. He had the most beautiful face I have ever seen. He seemed transfigured by the radiance of an inner light. There was a rare beauty in his eyes indicating he had grown old in years with gladness and with no indication that his mind had dimmed its lights.

Retirement—A New Adventure

Be sure that your mind never retires. It must be like a parachute that is no good unless it opens. Be open and receptive to new ideas. I have seen people of sixty-five and seventy retire. They seemed to rot away, and in a few months passed on. They obviously felt that life was at an end.

Retirement can be a new venture, a new challenge, a new path, the beginning of the fulfillment of a long dream. It is inexpressibly depressing to hear someone say, "What shall I do now that I am retired?" They are saying in effect, "I am mentally and physically dead. My mind is bankrupt of ideas."

All this is a false picture. The real truth is that you can accomplish more at ninety than you did at sixty, because each day you are growing in wisdom and understanding of life and the universe through your new studies and interest.

An executive who lives near me was forced to retire a few months ago because he had reached the age of sixty-five. He said to me, "I look upon my retirement as promotion from kindergarten to the first grade." He philosophized in this manner: He said that when he left high school, he went up the ladder by going to college. He realized this was a step forward in his education and understanding of life in general. Likewise, he added, now he could do the things he had always wanted to do, and, therefore, his retirement was still another step forward on the ladder of life and wisdom.

He came to the wise conclusion that he was no longer going to concentrate on making a living. Now he was going to give all his attention to living life. He is an amateur photographer, and he took additional courses on the subject. He took a trip around the world and took movies of famous places. He now lectures before various groups, lodges, and clubs, and is in popular demand.

There are countless ways of taking an interest in something worthwhile outside yourself. Become enthusiastic over new creative ideas, make spiritual progress, and continue to learn and grow. In this manner you remain young at heart, because you are hungering and thirsting after new truths, and your body will reflect your thinking at all times.

Secret of Youth

To recapture the days of your youth, feel the miraculous healing, self-renewing power of your subconscious mind moving through your whole being. Know and feel that you are inspired, lifted up, rejuvenated, revitalized, and recharged spiritually. You can bubble over with enthusiasm and joy, as in the days of your youth, for the simple reason that you can always mentally and emotionally recapture the joyous state.

The candle that shines upon your head is divine intelligence and reveals to you everything you need to know; it enables you to affirm the presence of your good, regardless of appearances. You walk by the guidance of your subconscious mind, because you know that the dawn appears and the shadows flee away.

Get a Vision

Instead of saying, "I am old," say, "I am wise in the way of the divine life." Don't let the corporation, newspapers, or statistics hold a picture before you of old age, declining years, decrepitude, senility, and uselessness. Reject it, for it is a lie. Refuse to be hypnotized by such propaganda. Affirm life—not death. Get a vision of yourself as happy, radiant, successful, serene, and powerful.

The Obstacle on Your Road to Happiness

Fear is humankind's worst enemy. It is the actual cause of many failures, diseases, and strained human relationships. Love will rout your fear. Love means an emotional commitment to the good things in life. Learn to love honesty, openness, justice, happiness, joy, and success. Live joyfully expecting the best and the best will become the deciding factor in your life.

Exercise: The Infallible Method to Overcome Any Fear

The following method for overcoming every fear has helped many people. It works like a charm. No matter if you are afraid of water, great heights, enclosed spaces, a lecture, or an interview, this method always helps.

Let's say you are afraid of swimming. Sit down in an armchair three or four times a day, completely relaxed, for five to ten minutes and imagine yourself swimming. In your fantasy you are actually swimming.

This is a subjective event: Using your imagination you place yourself in a swimming pool or a lake. You feel the cool water and the rhythmic movements of your arms and legs. You enjoy an activity that is fun for you. These aren't empty dreams, for you know each event in your fantasy will communicate itself to your subconscious. Sooner or later you will wish to realize the image that has been implanted into your subconscious. This is one of the principles of mind.

You can apply this technique to any fear. If you tend to quickly swoon, you only have to imagine yourself balancing on a narrow plank or climbing a mountain and enjoy the beautiful landscape far below yourself as well as your confident body control. The closer to reality these imaginings are, the faster the desired reaction will take place and make any fear disappear.

Insight into Practice

[Editor's note: At the end of each part of this book, you will find ways to put insight from this material into practice. These affirmations and meditations were originally part of a CD series based on this classic book by Dr. Joseph Murphy. The information has been transcribed for readers from the original. As with any meditation, practitioners may wish to use relaxing music or record the meditation and listen.]

Why is the life of one person overshadowed by illness and sadness but the life of another radiates with happiness? Why does one person enjoy wealth and renown while his neighbor is suffering from poverty and hardship? Through the laws of the mind, my message is simple: You are what you think daily—that is, what you think in your heart of hearts.

For everything you think, believe, and feel imprints itself into your subconscious. And your subconscious expresses everything with which you have imprinted on it in your personality and in your life. Therefore, it is crucial to think positively. For example, you should feed your subconscious with life-affirming and constructive thoughts and protect it from negative influences, no matter if they come from inside yourself or from an external source.

If you apply this principle daily, you can drastically change your life. You, too, can be healthy, vigorous, successful, and happy.

If you use this practical program, positive thinking will become an everyday matter of course, through which you can make use of the immeasurable powers of your subconscious—day by day, week by week. At the end of this section, you will find a relaxation exercise. Simply follow the instructions and let the words guide you, alone or with the accompaniment of some relaxing music of your choice.

By deeply relaxing, you let positive images anchor in your subconscious and change your life accordingly. Since a profound state of relaxation is crucial for good results, consider recording yourself reading the exercise aloud and then play it back as you complete the exercise, lying or sitting in a comfortable position with your eyes closed (not while driving, of course!).

Relaxation Exercise

Lie down comfortably on your back, legs stretched out next to each other, your arms loosely beside your body. Now find a comfortable position, move a little longer, feel your body. Are you really comfortable? If not, change your position until you feel truly at ease. And as soon as you have found your spot, take a moment. You want to relax deeply, here, in this place. That's why you should now close your eyes.

Everything around you sinks away, becomes unimportant. You forget your everyday life. You let everything happen that may come now. You're breathing calmly and regularly. You are breathing calmly and surrender to the moment. Lying like this, you feel that you are safe and secure. You lie comfortably on the ground, close to the ground, close to nature. You entrust yourself to it, you trustingly surrender. And you enjoy the pleasant feeling of wonderful relaxation: how nice it is to feel so safe and secure.

While your breathing grows more and more calm and deep, you travel deeper, become ever calmer. And you become aware of the silent point between breathing in and breathing out, the point of change where you breathe neither in nor out, and at that you just surrender. You're coming from breathing in and breathing out and certainly you will be coming again from breathing out to breathing in and you are happy about your body and how well it does it all by itself.

Let your breathing and the music, if you choose to play something relaxing, make you forget your routine. You surrender to the moment in which pleasant experiences are possible. You feel more and more relaxed and lighter with every breath. As light as you have always dreamed of being.

And while you're enjoying that cozy feeling of lightness, a beautiful summer landscape opens up to you. And while you continue to breathe calmly, you take a walk there in your mind and feel more and more comfortable. A soothing tranquility flows over you, your chest rises and sinks regularly, and breath for breath you arrive here where everything is light and peaceful.

You experience a moment of trusting surrender wholly within yourself where there is nothing left to do, nothing left to understand. Where everything is easy and natural, just as breathing regularly happens all by itself and you feel ever lighter, lighter and more pleasant with every time breathing out.

Yes, your journey into the world of your inner images is that easy and natural. Breath by breath your consciousness opens widely for the image of the summer landscape. You feel joy while you are looking over flowering meadows and cornfields, you find pleasure in every bush and tree and the sky. Calmly you breathe the fragrant summer air, let it fill your lungs. You breathe deeply and regularly and open up to the breath of nature, which pleasantly flows through your body.

Now you walk across a meadow, deeply and regularly you breathe in the mild summer air. You gather strength and admire the diversity of nature. The green of the plants and trees, the many colors of the flowers, the intense blue of the sky. In front of you glitters the burbling water of a little brook. Everything flows. Even the scent of the flowers flows over you.

You enjoy nature's breath. You want to linger here. A wonderful relaxedness now flows into your feet and legs. The relaxation wanders into your pelvis. Your pelvis is very relaxed, and simultaneously all the muscles of your belly region relax. You are filled by a warm, relaxing, pleasant feeling. It is as if the sun shone onto your belly while her warm rays scatter everywhere in your body. And in this manner the muscles in your chest and your trunk also relax.

Now the muscles in your shoulders relax. Relaxation reaches deeper and deeper levels. Now the muscles in your arms relax as well. Now the neck muscles; all the tension leaves your neck. The muscles grow soft and light. Now your facial muscles relax, your forehead, your cheeks, your eyes, the chin. All muscles of your face and head are completely relaxed.

You feel the state of wonderful, light relaxation in your whole body. You sit down in the soft grass, lean against the trunk of a tree. The tree is high and strong; leaning against its trunk you hear positive sentences that anchor deep in your subconscious. You feel happy and are connected to yourself and to life. You can change your life at any point. All you have to do is to change your thoughts and your beliefs. That will also change your feelings. From now on, only you will decide what you think. You will always choose that which is uplifting and life-affirming.

From now on you will think positively. You have decided to win in your life. You love yourself without condition. You make the best of yourself. Courageously you accept the challenges of life. You will make it. You forgive yourself for what you have done wrong so far. Also, you forgive all those who may have hurt you in the past. You wish peace, harmony, and every blessing of life on all people. You are full of life. You are full of energy, inspiration, and vigor.

You smile often, you are merry inwardly as well as outwardly. You have a good aura. You are very special. You feel well. You are conscious of your inner worth. You believe in yourself. It is beautiful to be alive and you are grateful for it.

And as you hear these sentences once more, you become aware of the positive feeling you experience with them. You can change your life at any point. All you have to do is to change your thoughts and your beliefs. That will also change your feelings. From now on, only you will decide what you think. You will always choose whatever is uplifting and life-affirming. From now on you will think positively. You have decided to win in your life. You love yourself without condition. You make the best of yourself. Courageously you accept the challenges of life. You will make it. You forgive yourself for what you have done wrong so far. Also, you forgive all those who may have hurt you in the past. You wish peace, harmony, and every blessing of life on all people.

You are full of life. You are full of energy, inspiration, and vigor. You smile often, you are merry inwardly as well as outwardly. You have a good aura. You are very special. You feel well. You are conscious of your inner worth. You believe in yourself. It is beautiful to be alive and you are grateful for it.

Gradually the summer landscape fades, the pictures retract. You are detached and free, balanced and harmonious. Slowly you return to your waking consciousness. You grow more and more alert. Your regular breath carries you back into the reality of space and time. Nice, isn't it, how relaxed and harmonious you feel. You're growing ever more alert. Move your hands and arms, legs and feet and stretch for a bit. Open your eyes. You feel calm and relaxed and harmonious. Enjoy your inner harmony.

The Subliminal Affirmations

You can tap the power of your subconscious in the best possible way. Record yourself reading the following affirmations out loud and listen to them with relaxing music to strengthen your self-confidence.

- I can change my life at any time.
- All I have to do is to change my thoughts and my beliefs.
- This will also change my feelings.
- From now on only I will decide what I'm thinking.
- I will always choose what is life-affirming and constructive.

- From this very moment I alone will decide what I think.
- I have decided to win in my life.
- I will make the best of myself.
- I courageously accept life's challenges.
- I will make it.
- I forgive myself what I have done wrong so far.
- I also forgive all people who may have hurt me in the past.
- I will forget the past. I am looking forward.
- I wish peace, harmony, and the blessings of life on all people. My views and convictions are constructive.
- In this way the power of my subconscious opens every door for me.
- It is good to be alive and I am grateful for it.

PART II

Health and Well-Being

Negative thoughts can often express themselves in the form of disturbances of well-being and health. Quite often, gastric ulcers, heart problems, or other symptoms mirror your mindset and emotional state. Your subconscious governs all the vital functions in your body at any time and independently of your conscious mind. If your bodily functions are in turmoil because of stress, sorrow, or negative thoughts, it is possible to restore your physical harmony through relaxation and positive suggestions.

This part of the book will help you with positive imaginings to activate your self-healing powers. If you are ill, you can support the treatment of a doctor or alterna-

tive practitioner in this way. And you can preserve your health by using the methods that are suggested here.

[Note that relaxation and positive thinking are no substitute for proper medical treatment. The meditation and relaxation techniques presented in this part are intended to be used as complementary therapies in support of professional medical care.]

CHAPTER FOUR

The Subliminal Messages

This part of the book builds on the following affirmations. Do you feel the strength and the positive energy that courses through you when you read these statements with awareness?

- I am healthy, whole, and complete.
- The more relaxed I am, the more stable my health will be.
- The power of my thoughts strengthens the balance of my body and soul.
- My positive thoughts and feelings strengthen my inner powers.
- Each cell of my body is awash with healing light.
- I love and accept myself.
- I am safe.
- Joy is coursing through me with each pulse of my life.

- I relax and joyfully let life take its course.
- Life inspires me and fills me with new energy.
- The harmony of nature is my companion in every breath.
- The power of my positive thinking makes me strong and healthy.
- Natural energy lends new strength to every cell of my body.
- I love and accept myself without condition.
- I decide to be healthy and free.

The Power of Your Subconscious in Your Healing

Your subconscious governs all the vital processes of your organism and knows the answer to every question. Whatever you imprint on your subconscious will appear as a situation, state, or event in your life. That's why you should carefully scrutinize the thoughts and imaginings of your conscious mind regarding their negative or positive content.

The power of your subconscious is enormous. It inspires you, it guides you, and it reveals to you names, facts, and scenes from the storehouse of memory. Your subconscious started your heartbeat, controls the circulation of your blood, and regulates your digestion, assimilation, and elimination. When you eat a piece of bread, your subconscious mind transmutes it into tissue, muscle, bone, and blood. This process is beyond the ken of the wisest man who walks the earth. Your subconscious mind controls all the vital processes and functions of your body and knows the answer to all problems.

Your subconscious mind never sleeps, never rests. It is always on the job. You can discover the miracle-working power of your subconscious by plainly stating to your subconscious prior to sleep that you wish a certain specific thing accomplished. You will be delighted to discover that forces within you will be released, leading to the desired result. Here, then, is a source of power and wisdom that places you in touch with omnipotence or the power that moves the world, guides the planets in their course, and causes the sun to shine.

Your subconscious mind is the source of your ideals, aspirations, and altruistic urges. It was through the subconscious mind that Shakespeare perceived great truths hidden from the average person of his day. Undoubtedly, it was the response of his subconscious mind that caused the Greek sculptor, Phidias, to portray beauty, order, symmetry, and proportion in marble and bronze. It enabled the Italian artist, Raphael, to paint Madonnas, and Ludwig van Beethoven to compose symphonies.

In 1955 I lectured at the Yoga Forest University in Rishikesh, India, and there I chatted with a visiting surgeon from Bombay. He told me about James Esdaile, a Scottish surgeon, who worked in Bengal before ether or other modern methods of anesthesia were discovered. Between 1843 and 1846, Dr. Esdaile performed about four hundred major operations of all kinds, such as amputations, removal of tumors and cancerous growths, as well as operations on the eye, ear, and throat. All operations were conducted under mental anesthesia only. This Indian doctor at Rishikesh informed me that the postoperative mortality rate of patients operated on by Dr. Esdaile was extremely low, probably 2 or 3 percent. Patients felt no pain, and there were no deaths during the operations.

Dr. Esdaile suggested to the subconscious minds of all his patients, who were in a hypnotic state, that no infection or septic condition would develop. You must remember that this was before Louis Pasteur, Joseph Lister, and others who pointed out the bacterial origin of disease and causes of infection due to unsterilized instruments and virulent organisms.

This Indian surgeon said that the reason for the low mortality rate and the general absence of infection, which was reduced to a minimum, was undoubtedly due to the suggestions of Dr. Esdaile to the subconscious minds of his patients. They responded according to the nature of his suggestion.

It is simply wonderful, when you conceive how a surgeon, almost two centuries ago, discovered the miraculous wonder-working powers of the subconscious mind. Doesn't it cause you to be seized with a sort of mystic awe when you stop and think of the transcendental powers of your subconscious mind?

Consider its extrasensory perceptions, such as its capacity for clairvoyance and clairaudience, its independence of time and space, its capacity to render you free from all pain and suffering, and its capacity to get the answer to all problems, be they what they may. All these and many more reveal to you that there is a power and an intelligence within you that far transcends your intellect, causing you to marvel at the wonders of it all. All these experiences cause you to rejoice and believe in the miracle-working powers of your own subconscious mind.

Example: A personal healing will be the most convincing evidence of the healing power of the subconscious mind. Over forty years ago I resolved a malignancy of the skin through prayer. Medical therapy had failed to check the growth, and it was getting progressively worse.

A clergyman, with a deep psychological knowledge, explained to me the inner meaning of the 139th

Psalm wherein it says, "In thy book all my members were written, which in continuance were fashioned, when as yet there was none of them."

He explained that the term *book* meant my subconscious mind, which fashioned and molded all my organs from an invisible cell. He also pointed out that inasmuch as my subconscious mind made my body, it could also re-create it and heal it according to the perfect pattern within it.

I prayed in a very simple way as follows: "My body and all its organs were created by the infinite intelligence in my subconscious mind. It knows how to heal me. Its wisdom fashioned all my organs, tissues, muscles, and bones. This infinite healing presence within me is now transforming every atom of my being making me whole and perfect now. I give thanks for the healing I know is taking place now. Wonderful are the works of the creative intelligence within me."

I prayed aloud for about five minutes, two or three times a day, repeating this simple prayer. In about three months my skin was whole and perfect.

As you can see, all I did was give life-giving patterns of wholeness, beauty, and perfection to my subconscious mind, thereby obliterating the negative images and patterns of thought lodged in my subconscious mind, which were the cause of all my trouble.

Nothing appears on your body except when the mental equivalent is first in your mind, and as you change your mind by drenching it with incessant affirmatives, you change your body.

Your Subconscious Is Your Book of Life

Whatever thoughts, beliefs, opinions, theories, or dogmas you write, engrave, or impress on your subconscious mind, you shall experience them as the objective manifestation of circumstances, conditions, and events. What you write on the inside, you will experience on the outside. You have two sides to your life, objective and subjective, visible and invisible, thought and its manifestation.

Your thought is received by your brain, which is the organ of your conscious reasoning mind. When your conscious or your objective mind accepts the thought completely, it is sent to the solar plexus, called the brain of your mind, where it becomes flesh and is made manifest in your experience.

As previously outlined, your subconscious cannot argue. It acts only from what you write on it. It accepts your verdict or the conclusions of your conscious mind as final. This is why you are always writing on the book of life, because your thoughts become your experiences. The American essayist, Ralph Waldo Emerson said, "Man is what he thinks all day long."

What Is Impressed in the Subconscious Is Expressed

William James, the father of American psychology, said that the power to move the world is in your subconscious mind. Your subconscious mind is one with infinite intelligence and boundless wisdom. It is fed by hidden springs and is called the law of life. Whatever you impress upon your subconscious mind, the latter will move heaven and earth to bring it to pass. You must, therefore, impress it with right ideas and constructive thoughts.

There is so much chaos and misery in the world because people do not understand the interaction of their conscious and subconscious minds. When these two principles work in accord, in concord, in peace, and synchronously together, you will have health, happiness, peace, and joy. There is no sickness or discord when the conscious and subconscious work together harmoniously and peacefully.

The tomb of Hermes was opened with great expectancy and a sense of wonder because people believed that the greatest secret of the ages was contained therein. The Hermetic axiom was as within, so without; as above, so below (referring to the spiritual world above and the physical world below as well as the soul within and the body without).

In other words, whatever is impressed in your sub-conscious mind is expressed on the screen of space. This same truth was proclaimed by Moses, Isaiah, Jesus, Buddha, Zoroaster, Lao Tzu, and all the illu-mined seers of the ages. Whatever you feel as true subjectively is expressed as conditions, experiences, and events. Motion and emotion must balance. As in heaven [your own mind], so on earth [in your body and environment]. This is the great law of life.

You will find throughout all nature the law of action and reaction, of rest and motion. These two must be in balance, then there will be harmony and equilibrium. You are here to let the life principle flow through you rhythmically and harmoniously. The intake and the outgo must be equal. The impression and the expression must be equal. All your frustra-tion is due to unfulfilled desire.

If you think negatively, destructively, and viciously, these thoughts generate destructive emotions, which must be expressed and find an outlet. These emotions, being of a negative nature, are frequently expressed as ulcers, heart trouble, tension, and anxieties.

What is your idea or feeling about yourself now? Every part of your being expresses that idea. Your vitality, body, financial status, friends, and social status represent a perfect reflection of the idea you have of yourself. This is the real meaning of what is impressed in your subconscious mind, and which is expressed in all phases of your life.

We injure ourselves by the negative ideas we entertain. How often have you wounded yourself by getting angry, fearful, jealous, or vengeful? These are the poisons that enter your subconscious mind. You were not born with these negative attitudes. Feed your subconscious mind life-giving thoughts, and you will wipe out all the negative patterns lodged therein. As you continue to do this, all the past will be wiped out and remembered no more.

How the Subconscious Controls All Functions of the Body

While you are awake or sound asleep upon your bed, the ceaseless, tireless action of your subconscious mind controls all the vital functions of your body without the help of your conscious mind. For example, while you are asleep, your heart continues to beat rhythmically, your lungs do not rest, and the process of inhalation and exhalation, whereby your blood absorbs fresh air, goes on just the same as when you are awake.

Your subconscious controls your digestive processes and glandular secretions, as well as all the other mysterious operations of your body. The hair on your face continues to grow whether you are asleep or awake. Scientists tell us that the skin secretes much more perspiration during sleep than during the waking hours. Your eyes, ears, and other senses are active during sleep. For instance, many of our great scientists have received answers to perplexing problems while they were asleep. They saw the answers in a dream.

Often your conscious mind interferes with the normal rhythm of the heart, lungs, and functioning of the stomach and intestines by worry, anxiety, fear, and depression. These patterns of thought interfere with the harmonious functioning of your subconscious mind.

When you are mentally disturbed, the best procedure is to let go, relax, and still the wheels of your thought processes. Speak to your subconscious mind, telling it to take over in peace, harmony, and divine order. You will find that all the functions of your body will become normal again. Be sure to speak to your subconscious mind with authority and conviction, and it will conform to your command.

Your subconscious seeks to preserve your life and restore you to health at all costs. It causes you to love your children, which also illustrates an instinctive desire to preserve all life. Let us suppose you accidentally ate some bad food. Your subconscious mind would cause you to regurgitate it. If you inadvertently took some poison, your subconscious powers would proceed to neutralize it. If you completely entrusted yourself to its wonder-working power, you would be entirely restored to health.

How to Get the Subconscious to Work for You

The first thing to realize is that your subconscious mind is always working. It is active night and day, whether you act upon it or not. Your subconscious is the builder of your body, but you cannot consciously perceive or hear that inner silent process. Your business is with your conscious mind and not your subconscious mind. Just keep your conscious mind busy with the expectation of the best, and make sure the thoughts you habitually think are based on whatsoever things are lovely, true, just, and of good report.

Begin now to take care of your conscious mind, knowing in your heart and soul that your subconscious mind is always expressing, reproducing, and manifesting according to your habitual thinking.

Remember, just as water takes the shape of the pipe it flows through, the life principle in you flows through you according to the nature of your thoughts. Claim that the healing presence in your subconscious is flowing through you as harmony, health, peace, joy, and abundance. Think of it as a living intelligence, a lovely companion on the way. Firmly believe it is continually flowing through you vivifying, inspiring, and prospering you. It will respond exactly this way. It is done unto you as you believe.

Example: There is the well-known, duly authenticated case of Madame Bire of France, recorded in the archives of the medical department of Lourdes, France. She was blind; the optic nerves were atrophied and useless. She visited Lourdes and had what she termed a miraculous healing.

Ruth Cranston, a Protestant young lady who investigated and wrote about healings at Lourdes in *McCall's* magazine, November 1955, wrote about Madame Bire as follows: "At Lourdes she regained her sight incredibly, with the optic nerves still lifeless and useless, as several doctors could testify after repeated examinations. A month later, upon reexamination, it was found that the seeing mechanism had been restored to normal. But at first, so far as medical examination could tell, she was seeing with 'dead eyes.'"

I have visited Lourdes several times where I, too, witnessed some healings, and, of course, as I shall explain in the next chapter, there is no doubt that healings take place at many shrines throughout the world, Christian and non-Christian.

Madame Bire was not healed by the waters of the shrine, but by her own subconscious mind, which responded to her belief. The healing principle within her subconscious mind responded to the nature of her thought. Belief is a thought in the subconscious mind. It means to accept something as true. The thought accepted executes itself automatically.

Undoubtedly, Madame Bire went to the shrine with expectancy and great faith, knowing in her heart she would receive a healing. Her subconscious mind responded accordingly, releasing the ever-present healing forces. The subconscious mind, which created the eye, can certainly bring a dead nerve back to life. What the creative principle created, it can re-create. According to your belief is it done unto you.

How to Convey the Idea of Perfect Health to Your Subconscious Mind

A Protestant minister I knew in Johannesburg, South Africa, told me the method he used to convey the idea of perfect health to his subconscious mind. He had cancer of the lung. His technique, as given to me in his own handwriting, is exactly as follows:

Several times a day I would make certain that I was completely relaxed mentally and physically. I relaxed my body by speaking to it as follows, "My feet are relaxed, my ankles are relaxed, my legs are relaxed, my abdominal muscles are relaxed, my heart and lungs are relaxed, my head is relaxed, my whole being is completely relaxed." After about five minutes I would be in a sleepy drowsy state, and then I affirmed the following truth, "The perfection of God is now being expressed through me. The idea of perfect health is now filling my subconscious mind. The image God has of me is a perfect image, and my subconscious mind recreates my body in perfect accordance with the perfect image held in the mind of God."

This minister had a remarkable healing. This is a simple, easy way of conveying the idea of perfect health to your subconscious mind.

Another wonderful way to convey the idea of health to your subconscious is through disciplined or scientific imagination. I told a man who was suffering from functional paralysis to make a vivid picture of himself walking around in his office, touching the desk, answering the telephone, and doing all the tasks he ordinarily would do if he were healed. I explained to him that this idea and mental picture of perfect health would be accepted by his subconscious mind.

He lived the role and actually felt himself back in the office. He knew that he was giving his subconscious mind something definite to work on. His subconscious mind was the film upon which the picture was impressed.

One day, after several weeks of frequent conditioning of the mind with this mental picture, the telephone rang by prearrangement and kept ringing while his wife and nurse were out. The telephone was about twelve feet away, but nevertheless he managed to answer it. He was healed at that hour. The healing power of his subconscious mind responded to his mental imagery, and a healing followed.

This man had a mental block that prevented impulses from the brain reaching his legs; therefore, he said he could not walk. When he shifted his attention to the healing power within him, the power flowed through his focused attention, enabling him to walk. "Whatsoever ye shall ask in prayer, believing, ye shall receive." Matthew 21:22

Harmony by the Power of Thought

Sorrow, fear, and worries can disturb the normal rhythm of your heart, your lungs, and other organs. Fill your subconscious with harmonic, healthy, and positive thoughts and soon all the functions of your organism will be normal once more. Accustom your consciousness with expecting only the best for you, and your subconscious will reliably let this image come true.

Exercise: Healthy While Sleeping

Your subconscious has formed your body and can also make you healthy. Fall asleep each night with the idea that you are completely healthy and that the most faithful of contractors, your subconscious, will carry out your order.

CHAPTER FIVE

The Healing Power of Your Subconscious in Practice

Your wish is your prayer. If you imagine with conviction that your wish has already come true, your prayer will be answered. Wish for reaching your goal in the easiest possible way—with the reliable aid of the principles of mind. You should experiment with the techniques that are introduced here until you have given yourself proof that the profound wisdom of your subconscious always reacts immediately to your conscious thoughts.

Mental Healings in Modern Times

Everyone is definitely concerned with the healing of bodily conditions and human affairs. What is it that heals? Where is this healing power? These are questions asked by everyone. The answer is that this healing power is in the subconscious mind of each person, and a changed mental attitude on the part of the sick person releases this healing power. No mental or religious science practitioner, psychologist, psychiatrist, or medical doctor ever healed a patient.

There is an old saying, "The doctor dresses the wound, but God heals it." The psychologist or psychiatrist proceeds to remove the mental blocks in the patient so that the healing principle may be released, restoring the patient to health. Likewise, the surgeon removes the physical block enabling the healing currents to function normally. No physician, surgeon, or mental science practitioner claims to have healed the patient.

The one healing power is called by many names—nature, life, God, creative intelligence, and subconscious power. As previously outlined, there are many different methods used to remove the mental, emotional, and physical blocks that inhibit the flow of the healing life principle animating all of us. The healing principle resident in your subconscious mind can and will, if properly directed by you or some other person, heal your mind and body of all disease.

This healing principle is operative in all of us regardless of creed, color, or race. You do not have to belong to some particular church in order to use and participate in this healing process. Your subconscious will heal the burn or cut on your hand even though you profess to be an atheist or agnostic. The modern mental therapeutic procedure is based on the truth that the infinite intelligence and power of your subconscious mind responds according to your faith.

The mental science practitioner or minister follows the injunction of the Bible—that is, the practitioner goes into the closet and shuts the door, stills the mind, relaxes, lets go, and thinks of the infinite healing presence within. They close the door of their mind to all outside distractions as well as appearances, and then they quietly and knowingly turn over their request or desire to their subconscious mind, realizing that the intelligence of their mind will answer them according to their specific needs.

The most wonderful thing to know is this: Imagine the end desired and feel its reality; then the infinite life principle will respond to your conscious choice and your conscious request. This is the meaning of belief you have received, and you shall receive. This is what the modern mental scientist does when they practice prayer therapy.

There is only one universal healing principle operating through everything—the cat, the dog, the tree, the grass, the wind, the earth—for everything is alive. This life principle operates through the animal, vegetable, and mineral kingdoms as instinct and the law of growth. Humankind is consciously aware of this life principle and can consciously direct it to bless themselves in countless ways.

There are many different approaches, techniques, and methods in using the universal power, but there is only one process of healing, which is faith, for according to your faith it is done unto you.

The Law of Belief

All religions of the world represent forms of belief, and these beliefs are explained in many ways. The law of life is belief. What do you believe about yourself, life, and the universe? It is done unto you as you believe.

Belief is a thought in your mind that causes the power of your subconscious to be distributed into all phases of your life according to your thinking habits. You must realize the Bible is not talking about your belief in some ritual, ceremony, form, institution, human, or formula. It is talking about belief itself. The belief of your mind is simply the thought of your mind. "If thou canst believe, all things are possible to him that believeth." Mark 9:23

It is foolish to believe in something to hurt or harm you. Remember, it is not the thing believed in that hurts or harms you, but the belief or thought in your mind that creates the result. All your experiences, all your actions, and all the events and circumstances of your life are but the reflections and reactions to your own thought.

What Does Prayer Therapy Mean?

Prayer therapy is the synchronized, harmonious, and intelligent function of the conscious and subconscious levels of mind specifically directed for a definite purpose. In scientific prayer or prayer therapy, you must know what you are doing and why you are doing it. You trust the law of healing. Prayer therapy is sometimes referred to as mental treatment, and another term is scientific prayer.

In prayer therapy you consciously choose a certain idea, mental picture, or plan you desire to experience. You realize your capacity to convey this idea or mental image to your subconscious by feeling the reality of the state assumed. As you remain faithful in your mental attitude, your prayer will be answered. Prayer therapy is a definite mental action for a definite specific purpose.

Let us suppose that you decide to heal a certain difficulty by prayer therapy. You are aware that your problem or sickness, whatever it may be, must be caused by negative thoughts charged with fear and lodged in your subconscious mind, and that if you can succeed in cleansing your mind of these thoughts, you will get a healing.

You, therefore, turn to the healing power within your own subconscious mind and remind yourself of its infinite power and intelligence and its capacity to heal all conditions. As you dwell on these truths, your fear will begin to dissolve, and the recollection of these truths also corrects the erroneous beliefs.

You give thanks for the healing that you know will come, and then you keep your mind off the difficulty until you feel guided, after an interval, to pray again. While you are praying, you absolutely refuse to give any power to the negative conditions or to admit for a second that the healing will not come. This attitude of mind brings about the harmonious union of the conscious and subconscious mind, which releases the healing power.

Subjective Faith and What It Means

You will recall the proposition, which need not be repeated at length, that your subjective or subconscious mind is as amenable to the control of your own conscious or objective mind as it is by the suggestions of another. It follows that whatever may be your objective belief, if you will assume to have faith actively or passively, your subconscious mind will be controlled by the suggestion, and your desire will be fulfilled. The faith required in mental healings is a purely subjective faith, and it is attainable upon the cessation of active opposition on the part of the objective or conscious mind.

In the healing of the body, it is, of course, desirable to secure the concurrent faith of both the conscious and subconscious mind. However, it is not always essential if you will enter into a state of passivity and receptivity by relaxing the mind and the body and getting into a sleepy state. In this drowsy state your passivity becomes receptive to subjective impression.

Example: I was asked by a man, "How is it that I got a healing through a minister? I did not believe what he said when he told me that there is no such thing as disease and that matter does not exist."

This man at first thought his intelligence was being insulted, and he protested against such a palpable absurdity. The explanation is simple. He was quieted by soothing words and told to get into a perfectly passive condition, to say nothing, and think of nothing for the time being. His minister also became passive, and affirmed quietly, peacefully, and constantly for about one-half hour that this man would have perfect health, peace, harmony, and wholeness. He felt immense relief and was restored to health.

It is easy to see that his subjective faith had been made manifest by his passivity under treatment, and the suggestions of perfect healthfulness by the minister were conveyed to his subconscious mind. The two subjective minds were then *en rapport*. The minister was not handicapped by antagonistic autosuggestions of the patient arising from objective doubt of the power of the healer or the correctness of the theory. In this sleepy, drowsy state, the man's conscious mind resistance was reduced to a minimum, and results followed. The subconscious mind of the patient being necessarily controlled by such suggestion exercised its functions in accordance therewith, and a healing followed.

The Meaning of Absent Treatment

Suppose you learned that your mother was sick in New York City and you lived in Los Angeles. Your mother would not be physically present where you are, but you could pray for her. It is the Father within which doeth the work.

The creative law of mind (subconscious mind) serves you and will do the work. Its response to you is automatic. Your treatment is for the purpose of inducing an inner realization of health and harmony in your mentality. This inner realization, acting through the subconscious mind, operates through your mother's subconscious mind as there is but one creative mind. Your thoughts of health, vitality, and perfection operate through the one universal subjective mind and set a law in motion on the subjective side of life, which manifests through her body as a healing.

In the mind principle there is no time or space. It is the same mind that operates through your mother no matter where she may be. In reality there is no absent treatment as opposed to present treatment, for the universal mind is omnipresent. You do not try to send out thoughts or hold a thought. Your treatment is a conscious movement of thought, and as you become conscious of the qualities of health, well-being, and relaxation, these qualities will be resurrected in the experience of your mother, and results will follow.

The following is a perfect example of what is called absent treatment. Recently, a listener of our radio program in Los Angeles prayed as follows for her mother in New York who had a coronary thrombosis:

The healing presence is right where my mother is. Her bodily condition is but a reflection of her thought-life like shadows cast on the screen. I know that in order to change the images on the screen I must change the projection reel. My mind is the projection reel, and I now project in my own mind the image of wholeness, harmony, and perfect health for my mother. The infinite heal-ing presence which created my mother's body and all her organs is now saturating every atom of her being, and a river of peace flows through every cell of her body. The doctors are divinely guided and directed, and whoever touches my mother is guided to do the right thing. I know that disease has no ultimate reality; if it had, no one could be healed. I now align myself with the infinite principle of love and life, and I know and decree that harmony, health, and peace are now being expressed in my mother's body.

She prayed in this manner several times daily, and her mother had a most remarkable recovery after a few days, much to the amazement of her specialist. He complimented her on her great faith in the power of God.

The conclusion arrived at in the daughter's mind set the creative law of mind in motion on the subjective side of life, which manifested itself through her mother's body as perfect health and harmony. What the daughter felt as true about her mother was simultaneously resurrected in the experience of her mother.

Example: A psychologist friend of mine told me that one of his lungs was infected. X-rays and analysis showed the presence of tuberculosis. At night before going to sleep he would quietly affirm, "Every cell, nerve, tissue, and muscle of my lungs are now being made whole, pure, and perfect. My whole body is being restored to health and harmony."

These are not his exact words, but they represent the essence of what he affirmed. A complete healing followed in about a month's time. Subsequent X-rays showed a perfect healing.

I wanted to know his method, so I asked him why he repeated the words prior to sleep. Here is his reply: "The kinetic action of the subconscious mind continues throughout your sleep-time period. Hence, give the subconscious mind something good to work on as you drop off into slumber." This was a very wise answer.

Practical Techniques in Mental Healings

An engineer has a technique and a process for building a bridge or an engine. Like the engineer, your mind also has a technique for governing, controlling, and directing your life. You must realize that methods and techniques are primary.

In building the Golden Gate Bridge, the chief engineer understood mathematical principles, stresses, and strains. Second, he had a picture of the ideal bridge across the bay. The third step was his application of tried and proven methods by which the principles were implemented until the bridge took form and we drive on it.

There also are techniques and methods by which your prayers are answered. If your prayer is answered, there is a way in which it is answered, and this is a scientific way. Nothing happens by chance. This is a world of law and order. In this chapter I present practical techniques for the unfolding and nurture of your spiritual life. Your prayers must not remain up in the air like a balloon. They must go somewhere and accomplish something in your life.

When we come to analyze prayer, we discover there are many different approaches and methods. We will not consider in this book the formal, ritual prayers used in religious services. These have an important place in group worship. We are immediately concerned with the methods of personal prayer as it is applied in your daily life and as it is used to help others.

Prayer is the formulation of an idea concerning something we wish to accomplish. Prayer is the soul's sincere desire. Your desire is your prayer. It comes out of your deepest needs and it reveals the things you want in life. Blessed are they who hunger and thirst after righteousness: for they shall be filled. That is really prayer—life's hunger and thirst for peace, harmony, health, joy, and all the other blessings of life.

The Passing-over Technique for Impregnating the Subconscious

This consists essentially in inducing the subconscious mind to take over your request as handed it by the conscious mind. This passing-over is best accomplished in the reverie-like state. Know that in your deeper mind is infinite intelligence and infinite power. Just calmly think over what you want; see it coming into fuller fruition from this moment forward.

Example: Be like the little girl who had a very bad cough and a sore throat. She declared firmly and repeatedly, "It is passing away now. It is passing away now." It passed away in about an hour. Use this technique with complete simplicity and naivete.

Your Subconscious Will Accept Your Blueprint

If you were building a new home for yourself and family, you know that you would be intensely interested in regard to the blueprint for your home; you would see to it that the builders conformed to the blueprint. You would watch the material and select only the best wood and steel, in fact, the best of everything.

What about your mental home and your mental blueprint for happiness and abundance? All your experiences and everything that enters into your life depend on the nature of the mental building blocks you use in the construction of your mental home.

If your blueprint is full of mental patterns of fear, worry, anxiety, or lack, and if you are despondent, doubtful, and cynical, then the texture of the mental material you are weaving into your mind will come forth as more toil, care, tension, anxiety, and limitation of all kinds.

The most fundamental and the most far-reaching activity in life is what you build into your mentality every waking hour. Your word is silent and invisible; nevertheless, it is real.

You are building your mental home all the time, and your thought and mental imagery represent your blueprint. Hour by hour, moment by moment, you can build radiant health, success, and happiness by the thoughts you think, the ideas you harbor, the beliefs you accept, and the scenes you rehearse in the hidden studio of your mind. This stately mansion, upon the construction of which you are perpetually engaged, is your personality, your identity in this plane, your whole life story on this earth.

Get a new blueprint; build silently by realizing peace, harmony, joy, and goodwill in the present moment. By dwelling upon these things and claiming them, your subconscious will accept your blueprint and bring all these things to pass. By their fruits ye shall know them.

The Science and Art of True Prayer

The term *science* means knowledge that is coordinated, arranged, and systematized. Let us think of the science and art of true prayer as it deals with the fundamental principles of life and the techniques and processes by which they can be demonstrated in your life, as well as in the life of every human being when they apply them faithfully. The art is your technique or process, and the science behind it is the definite response of creative mind to your mental picture or thought. "Ask, and it shall be given you; seek, and ye shall find; knock, and it shall be opened unto you." Matthew 7:7

Here you are told you shall receive what you ask for. It shall be opened to you when you knock, and you shall find what you are searching for. This teaching implies the definiteness of mental and spiritual laws. There is always a direct response from the infinite intelligence of your subconscious mind to your conscious thinking. If you ask for bread, you will not receive a stone.

You must ask believing, if you are to receive. Your mind moves from the thought to the thing. Unless there is first an image in the mind, it cannot move, for there would be nothing for it to move toward. Your prayer, which is your mental act, must be accepted as an image in your mind before the power from your subconscious will play upon it and make it productive. You must reach a point of acceptance in your mind— an unqualified and undisputed state of agreement.

This contemplation should be accompanied by a feeling of joy and restfulness in foreseeing the certain accomplishment of your desire. The sound basis for the art and science of true prayer is your knowledge and complete confidence that the movement of your conscious mind will gain a definite response from your subconscious mind, which is one with boundless wisdom and infinite power. By following this procedure, your prayers will be answered.

The Visualization Technique

The easiest and most obvious way to formulate an idea is to visualize it, to see it in your mind's eye as vividly as if it were alive. You can see with the naked eye only what already exists in the external world; in a similar way, what you can visualize in your mind's eye already exists in the invisible realms of your mind. Any picture you have in your mind is the substance of things hoped for and the evidence of things not seen. What you form in your imagination is as real as any part of your body. The idea and the thought are real and will one day appear in your objective world if you are faithful to your mental image.

This process of thinking forms impressions in your mind; these impressions in turn become manifested as facts and experiences in your life. The builder visualizes the type of building he wants; he sees it as he desires it to be completed. His imagery and thought processes become a plastic mold from which the building will emerge—a beautiful or an ugly one, a skyscraper or a very low one. His mental imagery is projected as it is drawn on paper. Eventually, the contractor and his workers gather the essential materials, and the building progresses until it stands finished, conforming perfectly to the mental patterns of the architect.

I use the visualization technique prior to speaking from the platform. I quiet the wheels of my mind so I may present to the subconscious mind my images of thought. Then I picture the entire auditorium and the seats filled with men and women, and each one of them illumined and inspired by the infinite healing presence within each one. I see them as radiant, happy, and free.

Having first built up the idea in my imagination, I quietly sustain it there as a mental picture while I imagine I hear men and women saying, "I am healed." "I feel wonderful." "I've had an instantaneous healing." "I'm transformed." I keep this up for about ten minutes or more, knowing and feeling that each person's mind and body are saturated with love, wholeness, beauty, and perfection. My awareness grows to the point where in my mind I can actually hear the voices of the multitude proclaiming their health and happiness; then I release the whole picture and go onto the platform. Almost every Sunday some people stop and say that their prayers were answered.

The Thank-you Technique

In the Bible, Paul recommends that we make known our requests with praise and thanksgiving. Some extraordinary results follow this simple method of prayer. The thankful heart is always close to the creative forces of the universe, causing countless blessings to flow toward it by the law of reciprocal relationship, based on a cosmic law of action and reaction.

For instance, a father promises his son a car for graduation; the boy has not yet received the car, but he is very thankful and happy, and is as joyous as though he had actually received the car. He knows his father will fulfill his promise, and he is full of gratitude and joy even though he has not yet received the car, objectively speaking. He has, however, received it with joy and thankfulness in his mind.

Example: I shall illustrate how Mr. Broke applied this technique with excellent results. He said, "Bills are piling up, I am out of work, I have three children and no money. What shall I do?" Regularly every night and morning, for a period of about three weeks, he repeated the words, "Thank you, Father, for my wealth," in a relaxed, peaceful manner until the feeling or mood of thankfulness dominated his mind. He imagined he was addressing the infinite power and intelligence within him knowing, of course, that he could not see the creative intelligence or infinite mind. He was seeing with the inner eye of spiritual perception, realizing that his thought-image of wealth was the first cause, relative to the money, position, and food he needed. His thought-feeling was the substance of wealth untrammeled by antecedent conditions of any kind.

By repeating, "Thank you, Father," over and over again, his mind and heart were lifted up to the point of acceptance, and when fear, thoughts of lack, poverty, and distress came into his mind, he would say, "Thank you, Father," as often as necessary. He knew that as he kept up the thankful attitude, he would recondition his mind to the idea of wealth, which is what happened.

The sequel to his prayer is very interesting. After praying in this manner, he met a former employer of his on the street whom he had not seen for twenty years. The man offered him a very lucrative position and advanced him money on a temporary loan. Today, Mr. Broke is vice president of the company. His recent remark to me was, "I shall never forget the wonders of 'Thank you, Father.' It has worked wonders for me."

The Affirmative Method

The effectiveness of an affirmation is determined largely by your understanding of the truth and the meaning of the words, "In praying use not vain repetition." Therefore, the power of your affirmation lies in the intelligent application of definite and specific positives. For example, a boy adds 3 and 3 and puts down 7 on the blackboard. The teacher affirms with mathematical certainty that 3 and 3 are 6; therefore, the boy changes his figures accordingly. The teacher's statement did not make 3 and 3 equal 6 because the latter was already a mathematical truth. The mathematical truth caused the boy to rearrange the figures on the blackboard.

It is abnormal to be sick; it is normal to be healthy. Health is the truth of your being. When you affirm health, harmony, and peace for yourself or another, and when you realize these are universal principles of your own being, you will rearrange the negative patterns of your subconscious mind based on your faith and understanding of whatever you affirm.

The result of the affirmative process of prayer depends on your conforming to the principles of life, regardless of appearances. Consider for a moment that there is a principle of mathematics and none of error; there is a principle of truth but none of dishonesty. There is a principle of intelligence but none of ignorance; there is a principle of harmony and none of discord. There is a principle of health but none of disease, and there is a principle of abundance but none of poverty.

I chose the affirmative method for use on my sister who was to be operated on for the removal of gallstones in a hospital in England. The condition described was based on the diagnosis of hospital tests and the usual X-ray procedures. She asked me to pray for her. We were separated geographically about 6,500 miles, but there is no time or space in the mind principle. Infinite mind or intelligence is present in its entirety at every point simultaneously.

I withdrew all thought from the contemplation of symptoms and from the corporeal personality altogether. I affirmed as follows:

This prayer is for my sister Catherine. She is relaxed and at peace, poised, balanced, serene, and calm. The healing intelligence of her sub-conscious mind which created her body is now transforming every cell, nerve, tissue, muscle, and bone of her being according to the perfect pattern of all organs lodged in her subconscious mind. Silently, quietly, all distorted thought patterns in her subconscious mind are removed and dissolved, and the vitality, wholeness, and beauty of the life principle are made manifest in every atom of her being. She is now open and receptive to the healing currents which are flow-ing through her like a river, restoring her to per-fect health, harmony, and peace. All distortions and ugly images are now washed away by the infinite ocean of love and peace flowing through her, and it is so.

I affirmed the prayer several times a day, and at the end of two weeks my sister had an examination that showed a remarkable healing, and the X-ray proved negative.

To affirm is to state that it is so, and as you main-tain this attitude of mind as true, regardless of all evi-dence to the contrary, you will receive an answer to your prayer. Your thought can only affirm, for even if you deny something, you are actually affirming the presence of what you deny. Repeating an affirmation, knowing what you are saying and why you are saying it, leads the mind to that state of consciousness where it accepts what you state as true. Keep on affirming the truths of life until you get the subconscious reaction that satisfies.

Visualize what is truly healing for you. Gain the firm conviction that your subconscious will let your body and soul recuperate if it is properly influenced. Envision the fulfillment of your wish in lively colors and see it as already come true. Whoever brings some stamina and concentration to the table won't have to wait long for success.

Exercise: Effective Prayer

Avoid any kind of forced mental effort while praying and don't try to enforce anything. Enter a semiconscious state and express in positive, uplifting terms what you want—in such a way as if it had already happened. Fall asleep confidently expecting that your prayer will be heard.

CHAPTER SIX

The Subconscious Serves Life

Your subconscious always serves life, but it can be influenced by your consciousness. Always present your subconscious with positive suppositions and true sets of facts and trust it to realize everything in your best interest.

The Tendency of the Subconscious Is Lifeward

Over 90 percent of your mental life is subconscious, so men and women who fail to make use of this marvelous power live within very narrow limits. Your subconscious processes are always lifeward and constructive. Your subconscious is the builder of your body and maintains all its vital functions. It is on the job twenty-four hours a day and never sleeps. It is always trying to help and protect you from harm.

Your subconscious mind is in touch with infinite life and boundless wisdom, and its impulses and ideas are always lifeward. The great aspirations, inspirations, and visions for a grander and nobler life spring from the subconscious. Your profoundest convictions are those you cannot argue about rationally because they do not come from your conscious mind; they come from your subconscious mind. Your subconscious speaks to you in intuitions, impulses, hunches, intimations, urges, and ideas, and it is always telling you to rise, transcend, grow, advance, adventure, and move forward to greater heights.

The urge to love, to save the lives of others comes from the depths of your subconscious. For example, during the great San Francisco earthquake and fire of April 18, 1906, people with disabilities, who had been confined to bed for long periods of time, rose up and performed some of the most amazing feats of bravery and endurance. The intense desire welled up within them to save others at all costs, and their subconscious responded accordingly.

Great artists, musicians, poets, speakers, and writers tune in with their subconscious powers and become animated and inspired. For example, Robert Louis Stevenson, before he went to sleep, used to charge his subconscious with the task of evolving stories for him while he slept. He was accustomed to ask his subconscious to give him a good, marketable thriller when his bank account was low. Stevenson said the intelligence of his deeper mind gave him the story piece by piece, like a serial. This shows how your subconscious will speak lofty and wise sayings through you, which your conscious mind knows nothing about.

Example: Mark Twain confided to the world on many occasions that he never worked in his life. All his humor and all his great writings were created because he tapped the inexhaustible reservoir of his subconscious mind.

How the Body Portrays the Workings of the Mind

The interaction of your conscious and subconscious mind requires a similar interaction between the corresponding system of nerves. The cerebrospinal system is the organ of the conscious mind, and the sympathetic system is the organ of the subconscious mind. The cerebrospinal system is the channel through which you receive conscious perception by means of your five physical senses and exercise control over the movement of your body. This system has its nerves in the brain, and it is the channel of your volitional and conscious mental action.

The sympathetic system, sometimes referred to as the involuntary nervous system, has its center in a ganglionic mass at the back of the stomach known as the solar plexus, and is sometimes spoken of as the abdominal brain. It is the channel of that mental action that unconsciously supports the vital functions of the body.

The two systems may work separately or synchronously. Judge Thomas Troward said this:

The vagus nerve passes out of the cerebral region as a portion of the voluntary system, and through it we control the vocal organs; then it passes onward to the thorax sending out branches to the heart and lungs; finally, passing through the diaphragm, it loses the outer coating which distinguishes the nerves of the voluntary system and becomes identified with those of the sympathetic system, so forming a connecting link between the two and making the man physically a single entity.

Similarly different areas of the brain indicate their connection with the objective and subjective activities of the mind respectively, and speaking in a general way we may assign the frontal portion of the brain to the former and the posterior portion to the latter, while the intermediate portion partakes of the character of both.

A rather simple way of looking at the mental and physical interaction is to realize that your conscious mind grasps an idea that induces a corresponding vibration in your voluntary system of nerves. This in turn causes a similar current to be generated in your involuntary system of nerves, thus handling the idea over to your subconscious mind, which is the creative medium. This is how your thoughts become things.

Every thought entertained by your conscious mind and accepted as true is sent by your brain to your solar plexus, the brain of your subconscious mind, to be made into your flesh, and to be brought forth into your world as a reality.

An Intelligence Takes Care of the Body

When you study the cellular system and the structure of the organs, such as eyes, ears, heart, liver, and bladder, you learn they consist of groups of cells that form a group intelligence whereby they function together and are able to take orders and carry them out in deductive function at the suggestion of the master mind (conscious mind).

A careful study of the single-celled organism shows what goes on in your complex body. Though the monocellular organism has no organs, it still gives evidence of mind action and reaction performing the basic functions of movement, alimentation, assimilation, and elimination.

Many say an intelligence will take care of your body if you let it alone. That is true, but the difficulty is that the conscious mind always interferes with its five-sense evidence based on outer appearances, leading to the sway of false beliefs, fears, and mere opinion. When fear, false beliefs, and negative patterns are made to register in your subconscious mind through psychological and emotional conditioning, there is no other course open to the subconscious mind except to act on the blueprint specifications offered it.

The Subconscious Mind Works for the Common Good

The subjective self within you works continuously for the general good, reflecting an innate principle of harmony behind all things. Your subconscious mind has its own will, and it is a very real something in itself. It acts night and day whether you act upon it or not. It is the builder of your body, but you cannot see, hear, or feel it building, as all this is a silent process. Your subconscious has a life of its own, which is always moving toward harmony, health, and peace. This is the divine norm within it seeking expression through you at all times.

How Man Interferes with the Innate Principle of Harmony

To think correctly, scientifically, we must know the truth. To know the truth is to be in harmony with the infinite intelligence and power of your subconscious mind, which is always moving lifeward. Every thought or action that is not harmonious, whether through ignorance or design, will result in discord and limitation of all kinds.

Scientists inform us that you build a new body every eleven months, so you are really only eleven months old from a physical standpoint. If you build defects back into your body by thoughts of fear, anger, jealousy, and ill will, you have no one to blame but yourself.

You are the sum total of your own thoughts. You can keep from entertaining negative thought and imagery. The way to get rid of darkness is with light; the way to overcome cold is with heat; the way to overcome the negative thought is to substitute the good thought. Affirm the good, and the bad will vanish.

Why It's Normal to Be Healthy, Vital, and Strong

The average child born into the world is perfectly healthy with all its organs functioning perfectly. This is the normal state, and we should remain healthy, vital, and strong. The instinct of self-preservation is the strongest instinct of your nature, and it constitutes a most potent, ever present, and constantly operative truth inherent in your nature. It is, therefore, obvious that all your thoughts, ideas, and beliefs must operate with greater potentiality when they are in harmony with the innate life principle in you, which is forever seeking to preserve and protect you along all lines. It follows that normal conditions can be restored with greater ease and certainty than abnormal conditions can be induced.

It is abnormal to be sick; it simply means you are going against the stream of life and thinking negatively. The law of life is the law of growth; all nature testifies to the operation of this law by silently, constantly expressing itself in the law of growth. Where there is growth and expression, there must be life; where there is life, there must be harmony, and where there is harmony, there is perfect health.

If your thought is in harmony with the creative principle of your subconscious mind, you are in tune with the innate principle of harmony. If you entertain thoughts that are not in accordance with the principle of harmony, these thoughts cling to you, harass you, worry you, and finally bring about disease, and, if persisted in, possibly death.

In the healing of disease, you must increase the inflow and distribution of the vital forces of your subconscious mind throughout your system. This can be done by eliminating thoughts of fear, worry, anxiety, jealousy, hatred, and every other destructive thought that tends to tear down and destroy your nerves and glands—body tissue that controls the elimination of all waste material.

Example: In the *Nautilus* magazine of March 1917, there appeared an article about a boy suffering from Pott's disease, or tuberculosis of the spine. He had a remarkable healing. His name was Frederick Elias Andrews of Indianapolis, and later minister of Unity School of Christianity in Kansas City, Missouri. His physician pronounced him incurable. The boy began to pray, and from a crooked, twisted cripple going about on hands and knees, he became a strong, straight, well-formed man. He created his own affirmation, mentally absorbing the qualities he needed.

He affirmed over and over again many times a day, "I am whole, perfect, strong, powerful, loving, harmonious, and happy." He persevered and said that this prayer was the last utterance on his lips at night and the first in the morning. He prayed for others also by sending out thoughts of love and health.

This attitude of mind and way of prayer returned to him multiplied many times. His faith and perseverance paid off with big dividends. When thoughts of fear, anger, jealousy, or envy drew his attention, he would immediately start his counteracting force of affirmation going in his mind. His subconscious mind responded according to the nature of his habitual thinking. This is the meaning of the statement in the Bible, "Go thy way, thy faith hath made thee whole." Mark 10:52

How Faith in Your Subconscious Powers Makes You Whole

A young man, who came to my lectures on the healing power of the subconscious mind, had severe eye trouble, which his doctor said necessitated an operation. He said to himself, "My subconscious made my eyes, and it can heal me."

Each night, as he went to sleep, he entered into a drowsy, meditative state, the condition akin to sleep. His attention was immobilized and focused on the eye doctor. He imagined the doctor was in front of him, and he plainly heard, or imagined he heard, the doctor saying to him, "A miracle has happened." He heard this over and over again every night for perhaps five minutes or so before going to sleep.

At the end of three weeks, he again went to the ophthalmologist who had previously examined his eyes, and the physician said to this man, "This is a miracle."

What happened? This man impressed his subconscious mind using the doctor as an instrument or a means of convincing it or conveying the idea. Through repetition, faith, and expectancy he impregnated his subconscious mind. His subconscious mind made his eye; within it was the perfect pattern, and immediately it proceeded to heal the eye. This is another example of how faith in the healing power of your subconscious can make you whole.

Your subconscious serves you. It has created your body and is active day and night. But you disturb its life-giving and preserving activity by negative thinking. Jealousy and fearful and sorrowful and hostile thoughts can attack nerves and glands and cause various mental and physical ailments. Therefore, you should avoid these kinds of thoughts.

Exercise: Healing Thoughts

As soon as you catch yourself thinking thoughts of jealousy, envy, or resentment, you should stop these monologues. Replace these unwholesome thoughts with thoughts of compassion, gratitude, and joy. Do this again and again. You will need a little patience for it until you experience at some point how miraculously this practice will change your life. Then you won't let thoughts of any other kind arise all by yourself.

Insight into Practice

Negative thoughts often express themselves in the form of disturbances in well-being and health. It isn't a rare phenomenon that gastric ulcers, heart problems, or other symptoms mirror your emotional state and mindset. The subconscious governs vital bodily functions at all times, independent of your consciousness. If your bodily functions are in turmoil as a result of stress, sorrow, and negative thoughts, it is possible to restore the harmony of your body through relaxation and positive suggestions.

This relaxation exercise will help you with positive imagery to activate your powers of self-healing. If you are ill, you can support the treatment of a doctor or an alternative practitioner in this way.

For best results, record yourself reading the exercise aloud and then play it back as you perform the exercise. Complete the exercise in a carpeted area or use an exercise pad or yoga mat for comfort.

Relaxation Exercise

Lie down comfortably on your back, legs stretched out next to each other, your arms loosely beside your body. Are you really comfortable? If not, change your position until you feel truly at ease. If you have found your spot like this, take a moment to arrive—just now, here on this floor that carries and supports you. You sink deeper and simultaneously you feel how you can just be here, in the inner world of your imagination.

Let this moment happen. Let good and profound experiences become possible. Everything around you sinks away, becomes unimportant. Let yourself be accompanied by your breathing and the music. You sink into a pleasant state of relaxation. You sink deeper and deeper.

Before your inner eye a beautiful summer day arises, a day as you have always dreamed of. You're lying on the beach of a lonely island, the sun is shining down from a clear blue sky, the sea is in front of you, the waves gently move up and down, up and down. The waves will take you into a state of pleasant relaxation, full of calmness and harmony.

The gentle breaking of the waves carries you deeper and deeper into relaxation, into peaceful dream images as you feel how your chest rises and falls to the rhythm of your breath, how your breath also is turning into a wave. You feel a gentle breeze on your forehead. It is pleasant to lie so relaxed on the warm sand. You feel that body and soul belong together and find their way to each other again.

And now you feel your chest and your abdomen. You feel how your breathing gently makes your abdominal wall rise and fall. And you sink ever more deeply into this wonderful relaxation. Your breathing rises and falls like waves, calmly and regularly, it happens all by itself. Each breath fills you with tranquility and warmth. With each breath a beautiful calmness flows through your body. Your breathing makes your abdominal wall rise and fall. With each exhalation you grow even more calm and relaxed.

Now imagine how you relax your body from head to toe. Relax your scalp and your entire head by employing your creative imagination. You feel how your head grows heavy and weary, and with each wave more so. Now relax your forehead and your facial muscles. While doing this, slightly open your mouth. The warmth of the sun's rays relaxes you even more deeply. Now imagine relaxing your neck and your shoulders. Now relaxation flows through your arms and hands in gentle waves. Now relax your back muscles, your pectoral muscles, the muscles of your abdomen; your breathing slowly makes the abdominal wall rise and fall. Let that pleasant relaxedness flow into your legs and into your toes. Your hips and legs relax and you feel how relaxation courses through your calves and feet and slowly reaches the toes.

It is a pleasant feeling to be so deeply relaxed. Every muscle and even the nerves are refreshingly relaxed. In this state of tranquility, the door to your subconscious can open widely, and each vision within yourself has a healing and empowering effect on you. And now we will go on a journey through your organs together. You will restore a healthy balance within your organism.

Hear and feel now how your heart is beating and thank it very kindly for all the countless times it has beaten already in your life. Imagine your heart pumping the blood regularly through your body while you're doing this. You feel how natural energy gives your body new strength. You feel the regular stream of this natural energy. And at the same time, you still breathe in and out regularly. And you enjoy the pleasant feeling.

Next, imagine your lungs. They are clear and bright. Vitality fills your lungs like a stream of healing energy. This energy cleans all the cells in your lungs and helps all the air sacs to take in even more oxygen. This fresh oxygen scatters throughout your whole body. Now your lungs feel the power of nature within them. And now you thank your lungs that they bring you new strength and vigor into your body every day, every minute, every second. And you feel the whole abundance of air and strength that is at your command, and when you breathe, you feel the whole vitality of your body.

Now direct your awareness to your stomach. Imagine your stomach how it absorbs and breaks down all the nourishment, how it takes in all the nutrients that are important for you. In this way your body is filled with new, vigorous life. And you see how your stomach shines with a bright light. The inner peace and harmony let a natural stream of energy course through your stomach. And now you lovingly thank it for its work and with that you feel the warmth in your belly.

Let your thoughts wander to your intestines and imagine them in a bright light. This healing light streams through your intestines and there it creates a wondrous harmony. A host of light particles flows from your stomach into your intestines and from there they flow through the whole body and nourish it with strength, light, and energy. And now you lovingly thank your intestines for their help.

Imagine your liver and your kidneys in the glorious colors of the rainbow, how they change everything the body doesn't need into beautiful colors. And you also thank your liver and kidneys for this miraculous transformation. And now you see how all your organs work together in love and harmony. You feel how the power of your imagination makes them all as well as yourself stronger and healthier.

Amazing, how intensely all the organs take up that message and how they restore the balance of body and soul. And you experience a wonderful, natural harmony with your body, in your heart, in your lungs, in your stomach and intestines, in your liver and your kidneys. With your positive thoughts and imaginings, you swim with the eternal stream of life, which heals you and lends you freedom, strength, and health. You enjoy life and feel a vigorous joy and love. Your whole body is filled with the forces of nature. You are healthy, totally and completely.

The more serene you are, the more stable your health will be. The power of your thoughts stabilizes the balance of your body and soul. Your positive thoughts and feelings strengthen your inner powers. Each cell of your body is awash with healing light. You love and accept yourself. You are safe. Joy courses through you with every pulsation of your life. You relax and cheerfully let life take its course. Life delights you and fills you with new energy. The harmony of nature accompanies you with every breath.

The power of your positive thinking gives you strength and health. Natural energy lends new strength to every cell of your body. Positive inner impulses make your body strong and vigorous. You unconditionally love and accept yourself. You decide to be free and healthy.

Slowly the images retreat, you are detached and free, balanced and in harmony. You slowly return to your waking consciousness. You grow more and more alert. Your regular breath carries you back into the reality of space and time. Nice, isn't it, how relaxed and harmonious you feel. You're growing ever more alert. Move your hands and arms, legs and feet and stretch for a bit. Open your eyes. You feel calm and relaxed and harmonious. Enjoy your inner harmony.

The Subliminal Affirmations

All of this subliminal information will flow into your subconscious while you are reading or listening. The following affirmations will strengthen your health and your well-being:

- I am healthy, whole, and complete.
- The more relaxed I am, the more stable my health will be.
- The power of my thoughts strengthens the balance of my body and soul.
- My positive thoughts and feeling strengthen my inner powers.
- Each cell of my body is awash with healing light.
- I love and accept myself.
- I am safe.
- Joy is coursing through me with each pulsation of my life.

- I relax and joyfully let life take its course.
- Life inspires me and fills me with new energy.
- The harmony of nature is my companion in every breath.
- The power of my positive thinking makes me strong and healthy.
- Natural energy lends new strength to every cell of my body.
- I love and accept myself without condition.
- I decide to be healthy and free.

PART III

Wealth and Success

It is an unwritten law that is valid in any time and place that our success in life is as high or low as our self-esteem. There is an immediate, causal connection between our way of thinking and the things we achieve. You can learn to develop a personal consciousness of wealth. You will feel more and more successful and wealthy. And soon you will be able to fulfill more and more of your wishes.

CHAPTER SEVEN

The Subliminal Messages

This part of the book discusses the following affirmations. Do you feel the strength and the positive energy that courses through you when you read these sentences with awareness?

- I am at one with the infinite wealth of my subconscious.
- I surround myself with wealth.
- I enjoy my wealth.
- I am successful.
- It is fun for me to give and to receive money.
- The more I give, the more I receive.
- I enjoy life, its great riches, and rewards.
- I have all the necessary skills to be successful.
- Whatever I need will spring forth from me.

- It is easy for me to make money.
- I enjoy my financial independence.
- I am growing more secure day by day.
- It is becoming easier for me to reach my financial goals.
- I enjoy dealing with money.
- I always have money to do and to have what I want.
- In every moment I am conscious of my true worth.
- My life turns into an experience of love and joy.

How You Realize Your Goals Using Your Subconscious

My message is simple: Decide to grow rich using the infallible power of your subconscious. Growing rich by hard work is a reliable method to end up in a coffin at an early age. It is unnecessary to waste your powers in this manner. Wealth is the consequence of a subconscious conviction. Make room for the idea to be wealthy in your thoughts and feelings.

If you are having financial difficulties, if you are trying to make ends meet, it means you have not convinced your subconscious mind that you will always have plenty and some to spare. You know men and women who work a few hours a week and make fabulous sums of money. They do not strive or slave hard. Do not believe the story that the only way you can become wealthy is by the sweat of your brow and hard labor. It is not so; the effortless way of life is the best. Do the thing you love to do, and do it for the joy and thrill of it.

Example: I know an executive in Los Angeles who receives a high salary. He went on a nine-month cruise seeing the world and its beauty spots. He said to me that he had succeeded in convincing his subconscious mind that he is worth that much money. He told me that many employees in his organization earning much less knew more about the business than he did, and could manage it better, but they had no ambition, no creative ideas, and were not interested in the wonders of their subconscious mind.

Wealth Is of the Mind

Wealth is simply a subconscious conviction on the part of the individual. You will not become a millionaire by saying, "I am a millionaire, I am a millionaire." You will grow into wealth consciousness by building into your mentality the idea of wealth and abundance.

The trouble with most people is that they have no invisible means of support. When business falls away, the stock market drops, or they lose their investments, they seem helpless. The reason for such insecurity is that they do not know how to tap the subconscious mind. They are unacquainted with the inexhaustible storehouse within.

Someone with a poverty-type mind finds themself in poverty-stricken conditions. Another person with a mind filled with ideas of wealth is surrounded with everything they need. It was never intended that we should lead a life of indigence. You can have wealth, everything you need, and plenty to spare. Your words have power to cleanse your mind of wrong ideas and to instill right ideas in their place.

Why Your Affirmations for Wealth Fail

I have talked to many people during the past thirty-five years whose usual complaint is, "I have said for weeks and months, 'I am wealthy, I am prosperous,' and nothing has happened." I discovered that when they said, "I am prosperous, I am wealthy," they felt within that they were lying to themselves. One man told me, "I have affirmed that I am prosperous until I am tired. Things are now worse. I knew when I made the statement that it was obviously not true."

His statements were rejected by the conscious mind, and the very opposite of what he outwardly affirmed and claimed was made manifest.

Your affirmation succeeds best when it is specific and when it does not produce a mental conflict or argument; hence, the statements expressed by this man made matters worse because they suggested his lack. Your subconscious accepts what you really feel to be true, not just idle words or statements. The dominant idea or belief is always accepted by the subconscious mind.

Example: I suggested to one businessman whose sales and finances were very low and who was greatly worried that he sit down in his office, become quiet, and repeat this statement over and over: "My sales are improving every day." This statement engaged the cooperation of the conscious and subconscious mind; results followed.

Don't Sign Blank Checks

You sign blank checks when you make such statements as, "There is not enough to go around." "There is a shortage." "I will lose the house because of the mortgage." If you are full of fear about the future, you are also writing a blank check and attracting negative conditions to you. Your subconscious mind takes your fear and negative statement as your request and proceeds in its own way to bring obstacles, delays, lack, and limitation into your life.

To him that hath the feeling of wealth, more wealth shall be added; to him that hath the feeling of lack, more lack shall be added. Your subconscious multiplies and magnifies whatever you deposit in it. Every morning as you awaken, deposit thoughts of prosperity, success, wealth, and peace. Dwell upon these concepts. Busy your mind with them as often as possible. These constructive thoughts will find their way as deposits in your subconscious mind and bring forth abundance and prosperity.

Your subconscious mind is never short of ideas. There are within it an infinite number of ideas ready to flow into your conscious mind and appear as cash in your pocketbook in countless ways. This process will continue to go on in your mind regardless of whether the stock market goes up or down, or whether the pound sterling or dollar drops in value. Your wealth is never truly dependent on bonds, stocks, or money in the bank; these are really only symbols necessary and useful, of course, but only symbols.

A Common Stumbling Block to Wealth

One emotion is the cause of the lack of wealth in the lives of many. Most people learn this the hard way. It is envy. For example, if you see a competitor depositing large sums of money in the bank, and you have only a meager amount to deposit, does it make you envious? The way to overcome this emotion is to say to yourself, "Isn't it wonderful. I rejoice in that man's prosperity. I wish for him greater and greater wealth."

To entertain envious thoughts is devastating because it places you in a very negative position; therefore, wealth flows *from* you instead of *to* you. If you are ever annoyed or irritated by the prosperity or great wealth of another, claim immediately that you truly wish for them greater wealth in every possible way. This will neutralize the negative thoughts in your mind and cause an ever greater measure of wealth to flow to you by the law of your own subconscious mind.

Rubbing Out a Great Mental Block to Wealth

If you are worried and critical about someone whom you claim is making money dishonestly, cease worrying about them. You know such a person is using the law of mind negatively; the law of mind takes care of those people. Be careful not to criticize them for the reasons previously indicated. Remember: the block or obstacle to wealth is in your own mind. You can now destroy that mental block. This you may do by getting on mental good terms with everyone.

Example: One of my students mailed me a newspaper clipping about a man called Ray Hammerstrom, a roller at the steel works in Pittsburgh operated by Jones and Laughlin Steel Corporation. He received $15,000 for his dream.

According to the article, the engineers could not fix a faulty switch in a newly installed bar mill that controlled the delivery of straight bars to the cooling beds. The engineers worked on the switch about eleven or twelve times to no avail.

Hammerstrom thought a lot about the problem and tried to figure out a new design that might work. Nothing worked. One afternoon he lay down for a nap, and prior to sleep he began to think about the answer to the switch problem. He had a dream in which a perfect design for the switch was portrayed. When he awoke, he sketched his new design according to the outline of his dream.

This visionary cat nap won Hammerstrom a check for $15,000, the largest award the firm ever gave an employee for a new idea.

How to Get the Results You Want

The principal reasons for failure are lack of confidence and too much effort. Many people block answers to their prayers by failing to fully comprehend the workings of their subconscious mind. When you know how your mind functions, you gain a measure of confidence. You must remember whenever your subconscious mind accepts an idea, it immediately begins to execute it. It uses all its mighty resources to that end and mobilizes all the mental and spiritual laws of your deeper mind. This law is true for good or bad ideas. Consequently, if you use it negatively, it brings trouble, failure, and confusion. When you use it constructively, it brings guidance, freedom, and peace of mind.

The right answer is inevitable when your thoughts are positive, constructive, and loving. From this it is perfectly obvious that the only thing you have to do to overcome failure is to get your subconscious to accept your idea or request by feeling its reality now, and the law of your mind will do the rest. Turn over your request with faith and confidence, and your subconscious will take over and answer for you.

You will always fail to get results by trying to use mental coercion—your subconscious mind does not respond to coercion; rather, it responds to your faith or conscious mind acceptance.

Your failure to get results may also arise from such statements as these: "Things are getting worse." "I will never get an answer." "I see no way out." "It is hopeless." "I don't know what to do." "I'm all mixed up." When you use such statements, you get no response or cooperation from your subconscious mind. Like a soldier marking time, you neither go forward nor backward; in other words, you don't get anywhere.

If you get into a taxi and give a half dozen different directions to the driver in five minutes, the driver would become hopelessly confused and probably would refuse to take you anywhere. It is the same when working with your subconscious mind. There must be a clear-cut idea in your mind. You must arrive at the definite decision that there is a way out, a solution to the vexing problem in sickness. Only the infinite intelligence within your subconscious knows the answer. When you come to that clear-cut conclusion in your conscious mind, your mind is then made up, and according to your belief is it done unto you.

Example: A homeowner once remonstrated with a furnace repairman for charging $200 for fixing the furnace. The mechanic said, "I charged five cents for the missing bolt and one hundred ninety-nine dollars and ninety-five cents for knowing what was wrong."

Similarly, your subconscious mind is the master mechanic, the all-wise one who knows ways and means of healing any organ of your body, as well as your affairs. Decree health, and your subconscious will establish it, but relaxation is the key. "Easy does it." Do not be concerned with details and means, but know the end result. Get the feel of the happy solution to your problem whether it is health, finances, or employment. Remember how you felt after you had recovered from a severe state of illness. Bear in mind that your feeling is the touchstone of all subconscious demonstration. Your new idea must be felt subjectively in a finished state, not in the future, but as coming about now.

In using your subconscious mind, you infer no opponent, you use no willpower. You imagine the end and the freedom state. You will find your intellect trying to get in the way, but persist in maintaining a simple, childlike, miracle-making faith. Picture yourself without the ailment or problem. Imagine the emotional accompaniment of the freedom state you crave. Cut out all red tape from the process. The simple way is the best.

Growing Rich–Almost Automatically

As you have read, relaxation is a crucial factor in letting your subconscious work for you in the best possible way. For this reason you should make use of the relaxation exercises I have presented in this book as often as possible.

In a state resembling sleep, the conflict of conscious and subconscious mind is widely neutralized. For that reason it is recommended to work with affirmations at night before you go to sleep.

Exercise: How to Sleep Yourself Rich

Joyously imagine the fulfillment of your desire again and again before you go to sleep. After you lie down, relax by repeating the word *wealth* in utter calmness and with true feeling, again and again. Sleep with the word *wealth* on your lips, and you will be astonished by the effect. Wealth will flow to you in abundance from every direction. You can, of course, also work with the word *success*.

Your Right to Wealth

Why should you content yourself with the most basic necessities when you can use the power of your subconscious? In this chapter you will learn how you can make money your friend and constant companion. Your desire to be rich is nothing but the desire for a life that is more fulfilled, beautiful, and happy. This is a natural instinct. For that reason, your ambition is not only good but very good.

It is your right to be rich. You are here to lead an abundant life and be happy, radiant, and free. You should, therefore, have all the money you need to lead a full, happy, and prosperous life. You are here to grow, expand, and unfold spiritually, mentally, and materially. You have the inalienable right to fully develop and express yourself along all lines. You should surround yourself with beauty and luxury.

Money is a symbol of exchange. It means to you not only freedom from want, but beauty, luxury, abundance, and refinement. It is merely a symbol of the economic health of the nation. When your blood is circulating freely in your body, you are healthy. When money is circulating freely in your life, you are economically healthy. When people begin to hoard money, to put it away in tin boxes, and become charged with fear, there is economic illness.

Money has taken many forms as a medium of exchange down through the centuries, such as salt, beads, and trinkets of various kinds. In early times a man's wealth was determined by the number of sheep and oxen he had. Now we use currency, and other negotiable instruments, as it is much more convenient to write a check than carry sheep around with you to pay bills.

How to Walk the Royal Road to Riches

Knowledge of the powers of your subconscious mind is the means to the royal road to riches of all kinds—spiritual, mental, or financial. Students of the laws of mind believe and know definitely that regardless of economic situations, stock market fluctuation, depression, strikes, war, and other conditions or circumstances, they will always be amply supplied, regardless of what form money takes. The reason for this is that they have conveyed the idea of wealth to their subconscious mind, and it keeps them supplied wherever they may be. They have convinced themselves in their mind that money is forever flowing freely in their life and that there is always a wonderful surplus.

Should there be a financial collapse of government tomorrow and all their present holdings become valueless, as the German marks did after the First World War, they would still attract wealth and be cared for, regardless of the form the new currency took.

Example: As you read this chapter, you are probably saying, "I am worthy of a higher salary than I am receiving." I believe most people are inadequately compensated. Many reason people do not have more money, I believe, is that they are silently or openly condemning it. They refer to money as "filthy lucre" or "the love of money is the root of all evil." Another reason they do not prosper is that they have a sneaky subconscious feeling there is some virtue in poverty. This subconscious pattern may be due to early childhood training or superstition or be based on a false interpretation of scriptures.

Money and a Balanced Life

One time a man said to me, "I am broke. I do not like money. It is the root of all evil." These statements represent a confused, neurotic mind. Love of money to the exclusion of everything else will cause you to become lopsided and unbalanced. You are here to use your power or authority wisely. Some people crave power; others crave money.

If you set your heart on money exclusively and say, "Money is all I want; I am going to give all my attention to amassing money; nothing else matters," you can get money and attain a fortune, but you have forgotten that you are here to lead a balanced life. You must also satisfy the hunger for peace of mind, harmony, love, joy, and perfect health.

By making money your sole aim, you simply made a wrong choice. You thought that was all you wanted, but you found after all your efforts that it was not only the money you needed. You also desired true expression of your hidden talents, true place in life, beauty, and the joy of contributing to the welfare and success of others. By learning the laws of your subconscious mind, you could have a million dollars or many millions, if you wanted them, and still have peace of mind, harmony, perfect health, and perfect expression.

There is no virtue in poverty; it is a disease like any other mental disease. If you were physically ill, you would think there was something wrong with you. You would seek help and do something about the condition at once. Likewise, if you do not have money constantly circulating in your life, there is something radically wrong with you.

The urge of the life principle in you is toward growth, expansion, and the life more abundant. You are not here to live in a hovel, dress in rags, and go hungry. You should be happy, prosperous, and successful.

Cleanse your mind of all weird and superstitious beliefs about money. Do not ever regard money as evil or filthy. If you do, you cause it to take wings and fly away from you.

Remember that you lose what you condemn. You cannot attract what you criticize.

How the Scientific Thinker Looks at Money

Suppose, for example, you found gold, silver, lead, copper, or iron in the ground. Would you pronounce these things evil? All evil comes from a darkened understanding, from ignorance, from a false interpretation of life, and from misuse of the subconscious mind. Uranium, lead, or some other metal could have been used as a medium of exchange. We use paper bills, checks, nickel, and silver, so surely, these are not evil.

Physicists and chemists know today that the only difference between one metal and another is the number and rate of motion of electrons revolving around a central nucleus. They can now change one metal into another through a bombardment of the atoms in the powerful cyclotron. Gold under certain conditions becomes mercury. I believe that our modem scientists in the near future will be able to make gold, silver, and other metals synthetically in the chemical laboratory. The cost may be prohibitive now, but it can be done. I cannot imagine any intelligent person seeing anything evil in electrons, neutrons, protons, and isotopes.

The piece of paper in your pocket is composed of atoms and molecules with their electrons and protons arranged differently. Their number and rate of motion are different. That is the only way the paper differs from the silver in your pocket.

Example: Many years ago I met a young boy in Australia who wanted to become a physician and surgeon, but he had no money. I explained to him how a seed deposited in the soil attracts to itself everything necessary for its unfolding, and that all he had to do was to take a lesson from the seed and deposit the required idea in his subconscious mind.

For expenses, this young, brilliant boy used to clean out doctors' offices, wash windows, and do odd repair jobs. He told me that every night, as he went to sleep, he used to picture in his mind's eye a medical diploma on a wall with his name on it in big, bold letters. He used to clean and shine the framed diplomas in the medical building where he worked. It was not hard for him to engrave the image of a diploma in his mind and develop it there. Definite results followed as he persisted with his mental picture every night for about four months.

The sequel of this story was very interesting. One of the doctors took a great liking to this young boy and after training him in the art of sterilizing instruments, giving hypodermic injections, and other miscellaneous first-aid work, he employed him as a technical assistant in his office. The doctor later sent him to medical school at his own expense.

This young man became a prominent medical doctor in Montreal, Canada. He discovered the law of attraction by using his subconscious mind the right way. He operated an age-old law that says, "Having seen the end, you have willed the means to the realization of the end." The end in this case was to become a medical doctor.

This young man was able to imagine, see, and feel the reality of being a doctor. He lived with that idea, sustained it, nourished it, and loved it until through his imagination it penetrated the layers of his subconscious mind and became a conviction, thereby attracting to him everything necessary for the fulfillment of his dream.

Why Some People Do Not Get a Raise in Pay

If you are working in a large organization and you are silently thinking of and resenting the fact you are underpaid, that you are not appreciated, and that you deserve more money and greater recognition, you are subconsciously severing your ties with that organization. You are setting a law in motion, and the superintendent or manager will say to you, "We have to let you go." Actually, you dismissed yourself. The manager was simply the instrument through which your own negative mental state was confirmed. It was an example of the law of action and reaction. The action was your thought, and the reaction was the response of your subconscious mind.

I am sure you have heard people say, "That fellow has a racket." "She is a racketeer." "He is getting money dishonestly." "She is a faker." "I knew him when he had nothing." "He is a crook, a thief, and a swindler."

If you analyze the man (or woman) who talks like that, you discover he is usually in want or suffering from some financial or physical illness. Perhaps his former college friends went up the ladder of success and excelled him. Now he is bitter and envious of their progress. In many instances this is the cause of his downfall. Thinking negatively of these classmates and condemning their wealth causes the wealth and prosperity he is praying for to vanish and flee away. He is condemning the thing he is praying for.

He is praying two ways. On the one hand he is saying, "Wealth is flowing to me now," and in the next breath, silently or audibly, he is saying, "I resent that fellow's wealth." Always make it a special point to rejoice in the wealth of the other person.

Protect your Investments

If you are seeking wisdom regarding investments, or if you are worried about your stocks or bonds, quietly claim, "Infinite intelligence governs and watches over all my financial transactions, and whatsoever I do shall prosper." Do this frequently and you will find that your investments will be wise; moreover, you will be protected from loss, as you will be prompted to sell your securities or holdings before any loss accrues to you.

In large stores the management employs store detectives to prevent people from stealing. They catch a number of people every day trying to get something for nothing. All such people are living in the mental atmosphere of lack and limitation and are stealing from themselves peace, harmony, faith, honesty, integrity, goodwill, and confidence. Furthermore, they are attracting to themselves all manner of loss, such as loss of character, prestige, social status, and peace of mind.

These people lack faith in the source of supply and the understanding of how their minds work. If they would mentally call on the powers of their subconscious mind and claim that they are guided to their true expression, they would find work and constant supply. Then by honesty, integrity, and perseverance, they would become a credit to themselves and to society at large.

Your Constant Supply of Money

Recognizing the powers of your subconscious mind and the creative power of your thought or mental image is the way to opulence, freedom, and constant supply. Accept the abundant life in your own mind. Your mental acceptance and expectancy of wealth has its own mathematics and mechanics of expression. As you enter into the mood of opulence, all things necessary for the abundant life will come to pass.

The place to and from which money can flow freely is healthy in an economic sense. You should view money as a phenomenon that resembles the tides: Ebb and flood follow each other in constant change.

If there is ebb tide, the flood is imminent with absolute certainty. The knowledge of the principles of the subconscious will always bring you wealth, no matter which form this may take in your life. The following exercise will help you to experience wealth.

Exercise: Gaining the Right Attitude Regarding Money

Using this technique you can multiply your financial means. Frequently repeat every day: "I welcome money, I like it, I use it wisely, considerately, and for good reasons. I like to spend it hand over fist and miraculously it returns to me, multiplied. Not only is money something good, but something very good indeed. Money is flowing toward me from all sides in abundance. Using it, I will do many good and helpful things, that's why I am grateful for my material and mental treasures."

CHAPTER NINE

The Subconscious and Success

Being successful means living successfully. If you are at peace with yourself, if you are happy and contented and follow your favorite pursuits, you are a successful human being.

The Three Steps to Success

Let us discuss three steps to success: The first step to success is to find out the thing you love to do, then do it. Success is in loving your work. Although, if you are a psychiatrist, for example, it is not adequate for you to get a diploma and place it on the wall; you must keep up with the times, attend conventions, and continue studying the mind and its workings. The successful psychiatrist visits clinics and reads the latest scientific articles. In other words, you stay informed in the most advanced methods of alleviating human suffering. The successful psychiatrist or doctor must have the interest of the patients at heart.

Someone may say, "How can I put the first step into operation? I do not know what I should do." In such a case, pray for guidance as follows: "The infinite intelligence of my subconscious mind reveals to me my true place in life." Repeat this prayer quietly, positively, and lovingly to your deeper mind. As you persist with faith and confidence, the answer will come to you as a feeling, a hunch, or a tendency in a certain direction. It will come to you clearly and in peace, and as an inner silent awareness.

The second step to success is to specialize in some particular branch of work and know more about it than anyone else. For example, if a young man chooses chemistry as his profession, he should concentrate on one of the many branches in this field. He should give all of his time and attention to his chosen specialty. He should become sufficiently enthusiastic to try to know all there is available about his field; if possible, he should know more than anyone else. The young man should become ardently interested in his work and should desire to serve the world.

He that is greatest among you, let him become your servant. There is a great contrast in this attitude of mind in comparison to that of the person who only wants to make a living or just "get by." Getting by is not true success. Your motive must be greater, nobler, and more altruistic. You must serve others, thereby casting your bread upon the waters.

The third step is the most important one. You must be sure that the thing you want to do does not redound to your success only. Your desire must not be selfish; it must benefit humanity. The path of a complete circuit must be formed. In other words, your idea must go forth with the purpose of blessing or serving the world. It will then come back to you pressed down, shaken together, and running over. If it is to benefit you exclusively, the circle or complete circuit is not formed, and you may experience a short circuit in your life, which may consist of limitation or sickness.

The Measure of True Success

Some people may say, "But Mr. James made a fortune in selling fraudulent oil stock." Someone may seem to succeed for a while, but the money they obtained by fraud usually takes wings and flies away.

When we rob from another, we rob from ourselves, because we are in a mood of lack and limitation, which may manifest itself in our body, home life, and affairs. What we think and feel, we create. We create what we believe. Even though someone may have accumulated a fortune fraudulently, that person is not successful. There is no success without peace of mind. What good is accumulated wealth if you cannot sleep nights, are sick, or have a guilt complex?

Example: I knew a man in London who told me of his exploits. He had been a professional pickpocket and had amassed a large amount of money. He had a summer home in France and lived in a royal fashion in England. His story was that he was in constant dread of being arrested by Scotland Yard. He had many inner disorders, which were undoubtedly caused by his constant fear and deep-seated guilt complex. He knew he had done wrong.

This deep sense of guilt attracted all kinds of trouble to him. Subsequently, he voluntarily surrendered to the police and served a prison sentence. After his release from prison, he sought psychological and spiritual counsel and became transformed. He went to work and became an honest, law-abiding citizen. He found what he loved to do and was happy.

Successful people love their work and express themselves fully. Success is contingent upon a higher ideal than the mere accumulation of riches. The person of success is someone who possesses great psychological and spiritual understanding. Many of the great industrialists today depend on the correct use of their subconscious minds for their success.

There was an article published some years ago about Flagler, an oil magnate. He admitted that the secret of his success was his ability to see a project in its completion. For instance, in his case, he closed his eyes, imagined a big oil industry, saw trains running on tracks, heard whistles blowing, and saw smoke. Having seen and felt the fulfillment of his prayer, his subconscious mind brought about its realization. If you imagine an objective clearly, you will be provided with the necessities, in ways you know not of, through the wonder-working power of your subconscious mind.

In considering the three steps to success, you must never forget the underlying power of the creative forces of your subconscious mind. This is the energy in back of all steps in any plan of success. Your thought is creative. Thought fused with feeling becomes a subjective faith or belief, and according to your belief "be it done unto you." Matthew 9:29

A knowledge of a mighty force in you, which is capable of bringing to pass all your desires, gives you confidence and a sense of peace. Whatever your field of action may be, you should learn the laws of your subconscious mind. When you know how to apply the powers of your mind, and when you are expressing yourself fully and giving of your talents to others, you are on the sure path to true success. If you are about God's business, or any part of it, God, by His very nature, is for you, so who can be against you? With this understanding there is no power in heaven or on earth to withhold success from you.

Example: A movie actor told me that he had very little education, but he had a dream as a boy of becoming a successful movie actor. Out in the field mowing hay, driving the cows home, or even when milking them, he said, "I would constantly imagine I saw my name in big lights at a large theater. I kept this up for years until finally I ran away from home. I got extra jobs in the motion-picture field, and the day finally came when I saw my name in great big lights as I did when I was a boy." Then he added, "I know the power of sustained imagination to bring success."

Thirty years ago I knew a young pharmacist who was receiving a small salary each week plus commission on sales. "After twenty-five years," he said to me, "I will get a pension and retire."

I said to this young man, "Why don't you own your own store? Get out of this place. Raise your sights. Have a dream for your children. Maybe your son wants to be a doctor; perhaps your daughter desires to be a great musician."

His answer was that he had no money. He began to awaken to the fact that whatever he could conceive as true, he could give conception. The first step toward his goal was his awakening to the powers of his subconscious mind, which I briefly elaborated on for his benefit. His second step was his realization that if he could succeed in conveying an idea to his subconscious mind, the latter would somehow bring it to pass.

He began to imagine that he was in his own store. He mentally arranged the bottles, dispensed prescriptions, and imagined several clerks in the store waiting on customers. He also visualized a big bank balance. Mentally he worked in that imaginary store. Like a good actor, he lived the role. Act as though I am, and I will be. This pharmacist put himself wholeheartedly into the act, living, moving, and acting on the assumption that he owned the store.

The sequel was interesting. He was discharged from his position. He found new employment with a large chain store and became manager and, later on, district manager. He saved enough money in four years to provide a down payment on a drugstore of his own. He called it his "Dream Pharmacy."

"It was," he said, "exactly the store I saw in my imagination." He became a recognized success in his chosen field and was happy doing what he loved to do.

Using the Subconscious Mind in Business

Some years ago I gave a lecture to a group of business leaders on the powers of imagination and the subconscious mind. In this lecture I pointed out how Goethe used his imagination wisely when confronted with difficulties and predicaments.

His biographers point out that he was accustomed to filling many hours quietly holding imaginary conversations. It is well known that his custom was to imagine one of his friends before him in a chair answering him in the right way. In other words, if he were concerned over any problems, he imagined his friend giving him the right or appropriate answer, accompanied with the usual gestures and tonal qualities of the voice, and he made the entire imaginary scene as real and as vivid as possible.

One of the friends present at this lecture was a young stockbroker. He proceeded to adopt the technique of Goethe. He began to have mental, imaginary conversations with a multimillionaire banker friend of his who used to congratulate him on his wise and sound judgment and compliment him on his purchase of the right stocks. He used to dramatize this imaginary conversation until he had psychologically fixed it as a form of belief in his mind.

This broker's inner talking and controlled imagination certainly agreed with his aim, which was to make sound investments for his clients. His main purpose in life was to make money for his clients and to see them prosper financially by his wise counsel. He is still using his subconscious mind in his business, and he is a brilliant success in his field of endeavor.

Example: A young boy who was attending high school said to me, "I am getting very poor grades. My memory is failing. I do not know what is the matter." I discovered that the only thing wrong with this boy was his attitude, which was one of indifference and resentment toward some of his teachers and fellow students. I taught him how to use his subconscious mind, and how to succeed in his studies. He began to affirm certain truths several times a day and particularly at night prior to sleep, and also in the morning after awakening. These are the best times to impregnate the subconscious mind.

He affirmed as follows: "I realize that my subconscious mind is a storehouse of memory. It retains everything I read and hear from my teachers. I have a perfect memory, and the infinite intelligence in my subconscious mind constantly reveals to me everything I need to know at all my examinations, whether written or oral. I radiate love and goodwill to all my teachers and fellow students. I sincerely wish for them success and all good things."

This young man is now enjoying a greater freedom than he has ever known. He is now receiving all top grades.

How to Become Successful in Buying and Selling

In buying and selling, remember that your conscious mind is the starter and your subconscious mind is the motor. You must start the motor to enable it to perform its work. Your conscious mind is the dynamo that awakens the power of your subconscious mind.

The first step in conveying your clarified desire, idea, or image to the deeper mind is to relax, immobilize the attention, get still, and be quiet. This quiet, relaxed, and peaceful attitude of mind prevents extraneous matter and false ideas from interfering with your mental absorption of your ideal. Furthermore, in the quiet, passive, and receptive attitude of mind, effort is reduced to a minimum.

The second step is to begin to imagine the reality of that which you desire. For example, you may wish to buy a home, and in your relaxed state of mind affirm as follows: "The infinite intelligence of my subconscious mind is all wise. It reveals to me now the ideal home, which is central, ideal, in a lovely environment, meets with all my requirements, and is commensurate with my income. I am now turning this request over to my subconscious mind, and I know it responds according to the nature of my request. I release this request with absolute faith and confidence in the same way that a farmer deposits a seed in the ground, trusting implicitly in the laws of growth."

The answer to your prayer may come through an advertisement in the paper or through a friend, or you may be guided directly to a particular home, which is exactly what you are seeking. Your prayer may be answered in many ways. The principal knowledge, in which you may place your confidence, is that the answer always comes, provided you trust the working of your deeper mind.

You may wish to sell a home, land, or any kind of property. In private consultation with real estate brokers, I have told them of the way I sold my own home on Orlando Avenue in Los Angeles. Many of them have applied the technique I used with remarkable and speedy results.

I placed a sign that read "For sale by owner" in the yard in front of my home. The day after I said to myself as I was going to sleep, "Supposing you sold your house, what would you do?"

I answered my own question and I said, "I would take that sign down and throw it into the garage." In my imagination I took hold of the sign, pulled it from the ground, placed it on my shoulder, went to the garage, threw it on the floor, and said jokingly to the sign, "I don't need you anymore." I felt the inner satisfaction of it all, realizing it was finished.

The next day a man gave me a deposit of $1,000 and said to me, "Take your sign down. We will go into escrow now."

Immediately I pulled the sign up and took it to the garage. The outer action conformed to the inner. There is nothing new about this. As within, so without, meaning according to the image impressed on your subconscious mind, so it is on the objective screen of your life. The outside mirrors the inside. External action follows internal action.

Here is another very popular method used in selling homes, land, or any kind of property. Affirm slowly, quietly, and feelingly as follows: "Infinite intelligence attracts to me the buyer for this home who wants it and who prospers in it. This buyer is being sent to me by the creative intelligence of my subconscious mind, which makes no mistakes. This buyer may look at many other homes, but mine is the only one he wants and will buy, because he is guided by the infinite intelligence within him. I know the buyer is right, the time is right, and the price is right. Everything about it is right. The deeper currents of my subconscious mind are now in operation bringing both of us together in divine order. I know that it is so."

Remember always, that what you are seeking is also seeking you, and whenever you want to sell a home or property of any kind, there is always someone who wants what you have to offer. By using the powers of your subconscious mind correctly, you free your mind of all sense of competition and anxiety in buying and selling.

How She Succeeded in Getting What She Wanted

A young lady regularly came to my lectures and classes. She had to change buses three times; it took her one and a half hours each time to come to the lectures. In one lecture I explained how a young man who needed a car in his work received one.

She went home and experimented as outlined in my lecture. Here is her letter in part, narrating her application of my method, and published with her permission:

Dear Dr. Murphy:

This is how I received a Cadillac car—I wanted one to come to the lectures regularly. In my imagination I went through the identical process I would go through if I were actually driving a car. I went to the showroom, and the salesman took me for a ride in one. I also drove it several blocks. I claimed the Cadillac car as my own over and over again.

I kept the mental picture of getting into the car, driving it, feeling the upholstery, etc., consistently for over two weeks. Last week I drove to your lectures in a Cadillac. My uncle in Inglewood passed away, and left me his Cadillac and his entire estate.

A Success Technique Employed by Many Outstanding Executives and Business Leaders

Many prominent businesspeople quietly use the abstract term *success* over and over many times a day until they reach a conviction that success is theirs. They know that the idea of success contains all the essential elements of success. Likewise, you can begin now to repeat the word *success* to yourself with faith and conviction. Your subconscious mind will accept it as true of you, and you will be under a subconscious compulsion to succeed.

You are compelled to express your subjective beliefs, impressions, and convictions. What does success imply to you? You want, undoubtedly, to be successful in your home life and in your relationship with others. You wish to be outstanding in your chosen work or profession. You wish to possess a beautiful home and all the money you need to live comfortably and happily. You want to be successful in your prayer life and in your contact with the powers of your subconscious mind.

You are a businessperson also because you are in the business of living. Become a successful businessperson by imagining yourself doing what you long to do and possessing the things you long to possess. Become imaginative; mentally participate in the reality of the successful state. Make a habit of it. Go to sleep feeling successful every night, and perfectly satisfied, and you will eventually succeed in implanting the idea of success in your subconscious mind. Believe you were born to succeed, and wonders will happen as you pray.

Success isn't a matter of chance. As soon as you are able to form a clear picture of your goal, the power of your subconscious will produce the necessary prerequisites for its realization. Using the following exercise you can make a career step of yours happen—or reach any other goal.

Exercise: Your Fantasy Prepares Reality

If you are dreaming of a career advancement, you should mentally imagine how your employer, your boss or your life partner already congratulates you for this success. This image in your fantasy has to come as close to reality as possible: Hear the voice of the congratulator, see their gestures, and let the real feeling of this scene permeate you. Never tire of working with these imaginings—and your wish shall be heard.

Insight into Practice

It is an unwritten law that is valid in any time and place that our success in life is as high or low as our self-esteem. There is an immediate, causal connection between our way of thinking and the things we achieve. You can learn to develop a personal consciousness of wealth. You will feel more and more successful and wealthy. And soon you will be able to fulfill more and more of your wishes.

For best results, record yourself reading the following exercise aloud, and then play it back as you are performing the exercise.

Relaxation Exercise

Lie down comfortably on your back, legs stretched out next to each other, your arms loosely beside your body. Are you really comfortable? If not, change your position until you feel truly at ease. If you have found your spot like this, take a moment to arrive. You sink deeper and relax more and more while you are feeling an increasing warmth and heaviness. You are growing calmer, more detached and relaxed.

Let this moment happen and forget your everyday life. Listen within where profound experiences are possible. Before your inner eye, the image of a summer day is beginning to form. You lie at the seashore in the warm, soft sand. The waves of the sea carry you away into a wonderful relaxation. The light breaking of the waves brings you a more and more profound relaxation. Your breathing is becoming a wave. Your abdominal wall slowly rises and falls. You sink deeper into this wonderful relaxation.

Your breathing rises and falls like the waves. Each breath fills you with tranquility and warmth. With each breath a wonderful calmness flows through your body. And now imagine how you relax your body from head to toe. Your facial muscles relax, forehead, cheeks, eye area; every muscle of your face is completely relaxed. Slightly open your mouth. Now imagine how your neck muscles relax. Neck and shoulders relax. Your relaxation is growing more profound with every moment.

Now the muscles in your left arm relax. They are growing light and fully relaxed. The muscles of your right arm also relax. Now relaxation is spreading throughout your body. Your chest and abdominal muscles completely relax. You are filled by a warm and pleasant feeling. It is as if the sun was shining into your belly. Her warming rays scatter in your whole body. Now your left thigh relaxes and relaxation flows down into your left calf and into the feet. The muscles of your right thigh relax, then the right calf and the right foot.

And now you see with your mind's eye how you take a walk on the beach. You feel the warm, soft sand underneath your feet; you smell the gentle breeze of the sea. You hear its calm, regular murmur. You have time to look around. You are looking over the beach where you discover a beautiful white yacht, which is tied to a pier. And you know it is your very own yacht. The yacht of your dreams. It also is a symbol for your growing prosperity, for your ability to accomplish your desires more and more.

You walk toward the yacht and enter onto its deck. You feel the warm floor made of wood. The scent of the wood is pleasant. You feel the gentle rocking of the yacht. And now, as if by magic, the yacht is starting to move. A steady wind lets you glide gently and safely through the waves. It is a marvelous feeling. You hear how the water splashes against the planks, and as you're standing on your yacht like this, you feel that you're surrounded by wealth. And you know that it is easy to be successful and rich.

Look around on your dream yacht and you are reminded that there is abundance and wealth in the world. And you imprint it into your subconscious that wealth and abundance are natural states. Whatever you want or need, it is yours already. It is at your disposal. You only need to claim it for yourself. You are one with the infinite wealth of your subconscious. It is your right to be wealthy, happy, and successful. Money is coming to you abundantly from sources that will never run dry. Life is wonderful.

Now observe the beautiful scenery around you. You gaze over the ocean that is spread out in front of you. The rays of the sun glitter on its surface like a thousand diamonds. And deep down in your heart you feel how truly rich you are and how you have inherited the world with everything that's in it. And now you give thanks for all these blessings in your life and in nature around you. You enjoy the miracle of the deep blue sky, of the ocean, which stretches out into infinity. All this has been created to bring you joy and you claim your share of the world's riches. Enjoy this wonderful feeling of enjoying your wealth.

You will start to develop this inner feeling of wealth more and more in your life. Imagine how you see gold, silver, and jewels in a shop window. The treasure house of cosmic riches is now open, and joyfully you realize that you have a part in its abundance. You always have the money to do and to get what you want. The more money you share with others, the more it is flowing to you. It is fun for you to give and receive money. The more you give, the more you receive.

It is easy for you to make money. You enjoy your financial independence. With each day you are growing more confident, and it is easier for you to reach your financial goals. You enjoy life, its riches and its rewards. You have all the necessary talents and abilities to be successful. Whatever you need or want, it wells up from you. You develop the playful skills for winning. Your life is turning into an experience of love and joy. You always have the money to do and to get what you want. The more money you share with others, the more it is flowing to you.

And now the images start to slowly retreat, the colors fade. The relaxation slowly leaves your body. It dissipates like a cloud in the wind. And slowly you are growing ever more alert. The relaxedness recedes even further from your body. You feel light and free. You are growing more and more alert and awake. You feel fresh and rested, relaxed and light. You slowly open your eyes and feel completely alert and easy. It is good to be alive.

The Subliminal Affirmations

All of this subliminal information will flow into your subconscious while you are reading or listening. In this way you can make the best use of the power of your subconscious. The following affirmations will strengthen your consciousness of wealth and success:

- I am at one with the infinite wealth of my subconscious.
- I surround myself with wealth.
- I enjoy my wealth.
- I am successful.
- It is fun for me to give and to receive money.
- The more I give, the more I receive.
- I enjoy life, its great riches and rewards.
- I have all the necessary skills to be successful.
- Whatever I need will spring forth from me.
- It is easy for me to make money.
- I enjoy my financial independence.
- I am growing more secure day by day.
- It is becoming easier for me to reach my financial goals.
- I enjoy dealing with money.
- I always have money to do and to have what I want.
- In every moment I am conscious of my true worth.
- My life turns into an experience of love and joy.

PART IV
Harmonious Relationships

Your relationships with other people are first and foremost determined by the emotions you have toward yourself. To be able to enter into a harmonious and wholesome contact with others, it is important to first learn to like yourself and expect only the best of relationships with others.

You will soon be able to shape your relationships with other people in an ever more positive and rewarding way. No matter how your family ties, your contacts, and friendships may look at the moment, you will be able to lastingly improve your relationships by performing these exercises.

CHAPTER TEN

The Subliminal Messages

This final section of the book relies on the following affirmations. Do you feel the strength and the positive energy that courses through you when you read these sentences with awareness?

- I love myself without condition.
- I am aware of myself.
- I am cordial, upright, and kind.
- I like to give but I also enjoy receiving.
- I wish unto others what I wish unto myself.
- I deserve to experience lots of joy and fun in my life.
- Each day I am more aware of my relationship with others.
- It is easy for me to make friends.
- I respect these friendships.

- I am able to express my feelings toward others.
- I find something good in every person.
- I enjoy being in exchange with others, nurturing them and supporting them.
- I am able to state and carry through my opinion confidently.
- I like myself without condition.

Your Subconscious Mind and Harmonious Human Relations

Your subconscious resembles an archive in which your thoughts are recorded and saved for further use. Think positively about your neighbor, and in the end you will think positively about yourself. You mind is a truly creative medium. Whatever you feel or think about other people will come true in your own life. Whatever you want your fellow men to think about you, you must think about them.

In studying this book, you learn that your subconscious mind is a recording machine that faithfully reproduces whatever you impress upon it. This is one of the reasons for the application of the Golden Rule in human relations.

Matthew 7:12 says, "All things whatsoever ye would that anyone should do unto you, do ye even so to them." This quotation has outer and inner meanings. You are interested in its inner meaning from the standpoint of your subconscious mind, which is this: As you would that others should think about you, think you about them in like manner. As you would that others should feel about you, feel you also about them in like manner. As you would want others to act toward you, act you toward them in like manner.

For example, you may be polite and courteous to someone in your office, but when his back is turned, you are very critical and resentful toward him in your mind. Such negative thoughts are highly destructive to you. It is like taking poison. You are actually taking mental poisons that rob you of vitality, enthusiasm, strength, guidance, and goodwill. These negative thoughts and emotions sink down into your subconscious and cause all kinds of difficulties and maladies in your life.

"Judge not, that ye be not judged. For with what judgment ye judge, ye shall be judged: and with what measure ye mete, it shall be measured to you again." Matthew 7:1–2

A study of these verses and the application of the inner truths therein contained represent the real key to harmonious relations. To judge is to think, to arrive at a mental verdict or conclusion in your mind. The thought you have about the other person is your thought, because you are thinking it. Your thoughts are creative; therefore, you create in your own experience what you think and feel about the other person. It is also true that the suggestion you give to another, you give to yourself because your mind is the creative medium.

This is why it is said, "For with what judgment ye judge, ye shall be judged." When you know this law and the way your subconscious mind works, you are careful to think, feel, and act right toward the other. These verses teach you about the emancipation of humans and reveal to you the solution to your individual problems.

The good you do for others comes back to you in like measure, and the evil you do returns to you by the law of your own mind. If, for example, someone cheats and deceives another, he is actually cheating and deceiving himself. His sense of guilt and mood of loss inevitably will attract loss to him in some way, at some time. His subconscious records his mental act and reacts according to the mental intention or motivation.

Your subconscious mind is impersonal and unchanging, neither considering other people nor respecting religious affiliations or institutions of any kind. It is neither compassionate nor vindictive. The way you think, feel, and act toward others returns at last upon yourself.

Begin now to observe yourself. Observe your reactions to people, conditions, and circumstances. How do you respond to the events and news of the day? It makes no difference if all the other people were wrong and you alone were right. If the news disturbs you, it is your evil because your negative emotions robbed you of peace and harmony.

A woman wrote me about her husband, saying that he goes into a rage when he reads what certain newspaper columnists write in the newspaper. She added that this constant reaction of anger and suppressed rage on his part brought on bleeding ulcers, and his physician recommended an emotional reconditioning.

I invited this man to see me, and I explained to him the way his mind functions indicating how emotionally immature it was to get angry when others write articles with which he disapproves or disagrees.

He began to realize that he should give the writers freedom to express themselves even though the latter disagreed with him politically, religiously, or in any other way. In the same manner, the writers would give him freedom to write a letter to the newspaper disagreeing with their published statements. He learned that he could disagree without being disagreeable.

He awakened to the simple truth that it is never what a person says or does that affects him; it is his reaction to what is said or done that matters.

This explanation was the cure for this man, and he realized that with a little practice he could master his morning tantrums. His wife told me, subsequently, that he laughed at himself and also at what the columnists said. They no longer have power to disturb, annoy, and irritate him. His ulcers have disappeared due to his emotional poise and serenity.

Example: A private secretary was very bitter toward some of the other employees in her office because they were gossiping about her and, as she said, spreading vicious lies about her. She admitted that she did not like women. She said, "I hate women, but I like men." I discovered also that she spoke to the women who were under her in the office in a very haughty, imperious, and irritable tone of voice. She pointed out that they took a delight in making things difficult for her. There was a certain pomposity in her way of speaking, and I could see where her tone of voice would affect some people unpleasantly.

I suggested a process of prayer to this private secretary who hated women, explaining to her that when she began to identify herself with spiritual values and commenced to affirm the truths of life, her voice, mannerisms, and hatred of women would completely disappear. She was surprised to know that the emotion of hatred shows up in a person's speech, actions, in their writings, and in all phases of their life. She ceased reacting in the typical, resentful, and angry way. She established a pattern of prayer, which she practiced regularly, systematically, and conscientiously in the office.

The prayer was as follows: "I think, speak, and act lovingly, quietly, and peacefully. I now radiate love, peace, tolerance, and kindliness to all the girls who criticized me and gossiped about me. I anchor my thoughts on peace, harmony, and goodwill to all. Whenever I am about to react negatively, I say firmly to myself, 'I am going to think, speak, and act from the standpoint of the principle of harmony, health, and peace within myself.' Creative intelligence leads, rules, and guides me in all my ways."

The practice of this prayer transformed her life, and she found that all criticism and annoyance ceased. The other women became coworkers and friends along life's journey. She discovered that there is no one to change but herself.

His Inner Speech Held Back His Promotion

One day a salesman came to see me and described his difficulties in working with the sales manager of his organization. He had been with the company ten years and had received no promotion or recognition of any kind. He showed me his sales figures, which were greater proportionately than the other salespeople in the territory. He said that the sales manager did not

like him, that he was unjustly treated, and that at con-
ferences the manager was rude to him and, at times,
ridiculed his suggestions.

I explained that undoubtedly the cause was to a
great degree within himself, and that his concept and
belief about his superior bore witness to the reaction
of this man. The measure we mete shall be measured
to us again. His mental measure or concept of the sales
manager was that he was mean and cantankerous. He
was filled with bitterness and hostility toward the
executive. On his way to work he conducted a vigorous conversation with himself filled with criticism,
mental arguments, recriminations, and denunciations
of his sales manager.

What he gave out mentally, he was inevitably
bound to get back. This salesman realized that his
inner speech was highly destructive because of the
intensity and force of his silent thoughts and emotions,
and personally conducted mental condemnation and
vilification of the sales manager entered into his own
subconscious mind. This brought about the negative
response from his boss as well as creating many other
personal, physical, and emotional disorders.

He began to pray frequently as follows: "I am the
only thinker in my universe. I am responsible for
what I think about my boss. My sales manager is not
responsible for the way I think about him. I refuse to

give power to any person, place, or thing to annoy me or disturb me. I wish health, success, peace of mind, and happiness for my boss. I sincerely wish him well, and I know he is divinely guided in all his ways."

He repeated this prayer out loud slowly, quietly, and with feeling. Knowing that his mind is like a garden, and that whatever he plants in the garden will come forth like seeds after their kind, I also taught him to practice mental imagery prior to sleep in this way: He imagined that his sales manager was congratulating him on his fine work, on his zeal and enthusiasm, and on his wonderful response from customers. He felt the reality of all this, felt his handshake, heard the tone of his voice, and saw him smile. He made a real mental movie, dramatizing it to the best of his ability. Night after night he conducted this mental movie, knowing that his subconscious mind was the receptive plate on which his conscious imagery would be impressed.

Gradually by a process of what may be termed mental and spiritual osmosis, the impression was made on his subconscious mind, and the expression automatically came forth. The sales manager subsequently called him to San Francisco, congratulated him, and gave him a new assignment as division sales manager over one hundred salespeople with a big increase in salary. He had changed his concept and estimate of his boss, and the latter responded accordingly.

Becoming Emotionally Mature

What another person says or does cannot really annoy or irritate you except if you permit them to disturb you. The only way they can annoy you is through your own thought. For example, if you get angry, you have to go through four stages in your mind: You begin to think about what was said. You decide to get angry and generate an emotion of rage. Then, you decide to act. Perhaps, you talk back and react in kind. You see that the thought, emotion, reaction, and action all take place in your mind.

When you become emotionally mature, you do not respond negatively to the criticism and resentment of others. To do so would mean that you had descended to that state of low mental vibration and become one with the negative atmosphere of the other. Identify yourself with your aim in life, and do not permit any person, place, or thing to deflect you from your inner sense of peace, tranquility, and radiant health.

The Meaning of Love in Harmonious Human Relations

Sigmund Freud, the Austrian founder of psychoanalysis, said that unless the personality has love, it sickens and dies. Love includes understanding, goodwill, and respect for the divinity in the other person. The more love and goodwill you emanate and exude, the more comes back to you.

If you attack the other person's ego and bruise their self-esteem, you cannot gain their goodwill.

Recognize that every person wants to be loved and appreciated and made to feel important in the world. Realize that other people are conscious of their true worth, and that, like yourself, they feel the dignity of being an expression of the one life principle animating all of us. As you do this consciously and knowingly, you build the other person up, and they, in turn, return your love and goodwill.

Handling Difficult People

There are difficult people in the world who are twisted and distorted mentally. They are malconditioned. Many are mental delinquents, argumentative, uncooperative, cantankerous, cynical, and sour on life. They are sick psychologically. Many people have deformed and distorted minds, probably warped during childhood. Many have congenital deformities.

You would not condemn a person who had tuberculosis, nor should you condemn a person who is mentally ill. No one, for example, hates or resents someone with a physical or mental illness. You should have compassion and understanding. To understand all is to forgive all.

Misery Loves Company

The hateful, frustrated, distorted, and twisted personality is out of tune with the infinite. He resents those who are peaceful, happy, and joyous. Usually he criticizes, condemns, and vilifies those who have been very good and kind to him. His attitude is this: Why should they be so happy when he is so miserable? He wants to drag them down to his own level. Misery loves company. When you understand this, you remain unmoved, calm, and dispassionate.

Example: An actor told me that the audience booed and hissed him on his first appearance on the stage. He added that the play was badly written and that undoubtedly he did not play a good role. He admitted openly to me that for months afterward he hated audiences. He called them dopes, dummies, stupid, ignorant, gullible, and so on. He quit the stage in disgust and went to work in a drugstore for a year.

One day a friend invited him to hear a lecture in New York City on "How to Get Along with Ourselves." This lecture changed his life. He went back to the stage and began to pray sincerely for the audience and himself. He poured out love and goodwill every night before appearing on the stage. He made it a habit to claim that the peace of God filled the hearts of all present, and that all present were lifted up and inspired. During each performance he sent out love vibrations to the audience.

He became a great actor, and he loves and respects people. His goodwill and esteem are transmitted to others and are felt by them.

The Practice of Empathy in Human Relations

A young woman who visited me stated that she hated another woman in her office. She gave as her reason that the other woman was prettier, happier, and wealthier than she and, in addition, was engaged to the boss of the company where they worked.

One day after the marriage had taken place, the daughter (by a former marriage) of the woman whom she hated came into the office. The child, who appeared to be disabled and had difficulty walking, put her arms around her mother and said, "Mommy, Mommy, I love my new daddy. Look what he gave me." She showed her mother a wonderful new toy.

She said to me, "My heart went out to that little girl, and I knew how happy she must feel. I got a vision of how happy this woman was. All of a sudden I felt love for her, and I went into the office and wished her all the happiness in the world, and I meant it."

In psychological circles today, this is called empathy, which simply means the imaginative projection of your mental attitude onto that of another. She projected her mental mood or the feeling of her heart into that of the other woman and began to think and look out through the other woman's mind. She was actually thinking and feeling as the other woman, and also as the child, because she likewise had projected herself into the mind of the child. She was looking out from that vantage point on the child's mother.

If you are prone to be envious, jealous, or angry, project yourself into the mind of Jesus and think from that standpoint, and you will feel the truth of the words, "Love ye one another."

Appeasement Never Wins

Do not permit people to take advantage of you and gain their point by temper tantrums, crying jags, or so-called heart attacks. These people are dictators who try to enslave you and make you do their bidding. Be firm but kind and refuse to yield. Appeasement never wins. Refuse to contribute to their delinquency, selfishness, and possessiveness. Remember, do that which is right. You are here to fulfill your ideal and remain true to the eternal verities and spiritual values of life, which are eternal.

Give no one in all the world the power to deflect you from your goal, your aim in life, which is to express your hidden talents to the world, to serve humanity, and to reveal more and more of God's wisdom, truth, and beauty to all people in the world. Remain true to your ideal. Know definitely and absolutely that whatever contributes to your peace, happiness, and fulfillment must of necessity bless all people who walk the earth. The harmony of the part is the harmony of the whole, for the whole is in the part, and the part is in the whole.

It isn't actually that difficult to lead loving and harmonious relationships. Just bring to mind: All you owe your neighbor is love. And love consists in nothing but wishing your neighbor what you are dreaming of for yourself: health, happiness, and contentment.

Exercise: Own Opinion

Pay heightened attention to how you are dealing with the fact that every person has the right to their own opinion as well as a right to express this opinion. Do you—in your emotional sphere—react like a mature person? Do you concede that your fellow human has this right? Even if you don't like that person's opinion? You can claim the same right for yourself. Can you preserve your point of view without getting rude or impolite over it?

CHAPTER ELEVEN

How to Forgive Others as Well as Yourself

The concept you have of God is a crucial foundation in your life. If you believe in a God of love, your subconscious will react accordingly and make you content. Life—or God—isn't resentful. Life won't judge anyone. Life heals serious physical injuries. It knows how to forgive if you burn your hand: it creates new cells, new tissue. Life will heal everything. In this chapter I address how you should learn to forgive yourself as well as others.

How to Use Your Subconscious Mind for Forgiveness

If you set up resistance in your mind to the flow of life through you, this emotional congestion will get snarled up in your subconscious mind and cause all kinds of negative conditions. God has nothing to do with unhappy or chaotic conditions in the world. All these conditions are brought about by humankind's negative and destructive thinking. Therefore, it is silly to blame God for your trouble or sickness.

Many people habitually set up mental resistance to the flow of life by accusing and reproaching God for the sin, sickness, and suffering of humanity. As long as people entertain such negative concepts about God, they will experience the automatic negative reactions from their subconscious minds. Actually, such people do not know that they are punishing themselves. They must see the truth, find release, and give up all condemnation, resentment, and anger against anyone or any power outside themselves. Otherwise, they cannot go forward into a healthy, happy, or creative activity.

The minute these people entertain a God of love in their minds and hearts, and when they believe that God is their Loving Father who watches over them, cares for them, guides them, sustains and strengthens them, this concept and belief about God or the life principle will be accepted by their subconscious mind, and they will find themselves blessed in countless ways.

Life Always Forgives You

Life forgives you when you cut your finger. The subconscious intelligence within you sets about immediately to repair it. New cells build bridges over the cut. Should you take some tainted food by error, life forgives you and causes you to regurgitate it in order to preserve you. If you burn your hand, the life principle reduces the edema and congestion and gives you new skin, tissue, and cells. Life holds no grudges against you and is always forgiving you.

Life brings you back to health, vitality, harmony, and peace, if you cooperate by thinking in harmony with nature. Negative, hurtful memories, bitterness, and ill will clutter up and impede the free flow of the life principle in you.

I knew a man who worked every night until about one o'clock in the morning. He paid no attention to his two boys or his wife. He was always too busy working hard. He thought people should pat him on the back because he was working so arduously and persistently past midnight every night. He had a blood pressure of over 200 and was full of guilt. Unconsciously, he proceeded to punish himself by hard work. A normal man does not do that. He is interested in his children and in their development. He does not shut his wife out of his world.

I explained to him why he was working so arduously: "There is something eating you inside; otherwise, you would not act this way. You are punishing yourself, and you have to learn to forgive yourself."

He did have a deep sense of guilt. It was toward a brother.

I explained to him that God was not punishing him, but that he was punishing himself. For example, if you misuse the laws of life, you will suffer accordingly. If you put your hand on a charged wire, you will get burned. The forces of nature are not evil; it is your use of them that determines whether they have a good or evil effect. Electricity is not evil; it depends on how you use it, whether to burn down a structure or light up a home. The only sin is ignorance of the law, and the only punishment is the automatic reaction of our misuse of the law.

If you misuse the principle of chemistry, you may blow up the office or the factory. If you strike your hand on a board, you may cause your hand to bleed. The board is not for that purpose. Its purpose may be to lean upon or to support your feet.

This man realized that God does not condemn or punish anyone, and that all his suffering was due to the reaction of his subconscious mind to his own negative and destructive thinking. He had cheated his brother at one time, and the brother had now passed on. Still, he was full of remorse and guilt.

I asked him, "Would you cheat your brother now?"

He said, "No."

"Did you feel you were justified at the time?"

His reply was, "Yes."

"But you would not do it now?"

He added, "No, I am helping others to know how to live."

I added the following comment: "You have a greater reason and understanding now. Forgiveness is to forgive yourself. Forgiveness is getting your thoughts in line with the divine law of harmony. Self-condemnation is called hell (bondage and restriction); forgiveness is called heaven (harmony and peace)."

The burden of guilt and self-condemnation was lifted from his mind, and he had a complete healing. The doctor tested his blood pressure, and it had become normal. The explanation was the cure.

Criticism Cannot Hurt You Without Your Consent

A schoolteacher told me that one of her associates had written her a letter criticizing a speech she had given. In the letter, the associate stated that the teacher spoke too fast, swallowed some of her words, and couldn't be heard; furthermore, her diction was poor, and her speech ineffective. This teacher was furious and full of resentment toward her critic.

She admitted to me that the criticisms were just. Her first reaction was really childish, and she agreed that the criticism was really a blessing and a marvelous corrective. She proceeded immediately to supplement her deficiencies in her speech by enrolling in a course in public speaking at a college. She wrote and thanked the writer of the note for her interest, expressing appreciation for her conclusions and findings, which enabled the teacher to correct the matter at once.

Suppose none of the things mentioned in the letter had been true of the teacher. The latter would have realized that her class material had upset the prejudices, superstitions, or narrow sectarian beliefs of the writer of the note, and that a psychologically ill person was simply pouring forth her resentment because a psychological boil had been hurt.

To understand this fact is to be compassionate. The next logical step would be to pray for the other person's peace, harmony, and understanding. You cannot be hurt when you know that you are master of your thoughts, reactions, and emotions. Emotions follow thoughts, and you have the power to reject all thoughts that may disturb or upset you.

Forgiveness Is Necessary for Healing

"And when ye stand praying, forgive, if ye have ought against any." Mark 11:25

Forgiveness of others is essential to mental peace and radiant health. You must forgive everyone who has ever hurt you if you want perfect health and happiness. Forgive yourself by getting your thoughts in harmony with divine law and order. You cannot really forgive yourself completely until you have forgiven others first. To refuse to forgive yourself is nothing more or less than spiritual pride or ignorance.

In the psychosomatic field of medicine today, it is being constantly stressed that resentment, condemnation of others, remorse, and hostility are behind a host of maladies ranging from arthritis to cardiac disease. Practitioners point out that these sick people, who were hurt, mistreated, deceived, or injured, were full of resentment and hatred for those who hurt them. This caused inflamed and festering wounds in their subconscious minds, There is only one remedy. They have to cut out and discard their hurts, and the one and only sure way is by forgiveness.

Example: Some years ago I visited a church to perform a marriage ceremony. The young man did not appear, and at the end of two hours, the bride-to-be shed a few tears, and then said to me, "I prayed for divine guidance. This might be the answer for He never faileth."

That was her reaction—faith in God and all things good. She had no bitterness in her heart because as she said, "It must not have been the right action because my prayer was for the right action for both of us."

Someone else having a similar experience would have gone into a tantrum, have had an emotional fit, required sedation, and perhaps needed hospital-ization.

Tune in with the infinite intelligence within your subconscious depths, trusting the answer in the same way that you trusted your mother when she held you in her arms. This is how you can acquire poise and mental and emotional health.

Forgiveness Is Love in Action

The essential ingredient in the art of forgiveness is the willingness to forgive. If you sincerely desire to forgive the other, you are 51 percent over the hurdle. I feel sure you know that to forgive the other does not necessarily mean that you like the person or want to associate with them. You cannot be compelled to like someone; neither can a government legislate good-will, love, peace, or tolerance. It is quite impossible to like people because someone in Washington issues an edict to that effect. We can, however, love people without liking them.

The Bible encourages us to love one another. This, anyone can do who really wants to do it. Love means that you wish for the other health, happiness, peace, joy, and all the blessings of life. There is only one prerequisite, and that is sincerity. You are not being magnanimous when you forgive; you are really being selfish, because what you wish for the other, you are actually wishing for yourself. The reason is that you are thinking it and you are feeling it. As you think and feel, so are you. Could anything be simpler than that?

The Acid Test for Forgiveness

There is an acid test for gold. There is also an acid test for forgiveness. If I should tell you something wonderful about someone who has wronged you, cheated you, or defrauded you, and you sizzled at hearing the good news about this person, the roots of hatred would still be in your subconscious mind, playing havoc with you.

Let us suppose you had a painful abscess on your jaw a year ago, and you told me about it. I would casually ask you if you had any pain now. You would automatically say, "Of course not, I have a memory of it but no pain." That is the whole story. You may have a memory of the incident but no sting or hurt anymore. This is the acid test, and you must meet it psychologically and spiritually; otherwise, you are simply deceiving yourself and not practicing the true art of forgiveness.

To Understand All Is to Forgive All

When you understand the creative law of your own mind, you cease to blame other people and conditions for making or marring your life. You know that your own thoughts and feelings create your destiny. Furthermore, you are aware that externals are not the causes and conditions of your life and your experiences. To think that others can mar your happiness, that you are the football of a cruel fate, that you must oppose and fight others for a living—all these and other thoughts like them are untenable when you understand that thoughts are things.

To forgive means to wish love, peace, joy, wisdom, and contentment for the other person until the memory has lost its sting. This is the litmus test of true forgiveness. Maybe you won't forget the insult or injury, but it won't hurt you anymore. The following exercise will help you to consciously forgive another person.

Exercise: The Technique of Forgiveness

If you apply the following simple technique, your life will change.

- Calm your thoughts and relax your body and mind.
- Think of God and His love for all people.
- Sincerely speak the words: "I forgive [insert the name of the person in question] fully and completely. I am free of bitterness. I forgive without any restriction everything that has happened to me in this matter. I am free of it and he (or she) is free. It is a wonderful feeling. Today is the day of a general

amnesty. I wish him (or her) and all fellow humans health, happiness, and complete contentment. I do this of my own free will, full of love and joy and as soon as the name of this person will come to my mind I will say: 'You are free of all guilt.' I am free, and you are free. May we all experience happiness and joy."

The great secret of true forgiveness is the fact the one single act of forgiveness is enough. As soon as the person in question or the iniquity caused by him or her reappears, it is enough to say: "Peace be with you." Do this every time the memory overcomes you. After a few days you will realize that your thoughts circle less and less around this person or this event until ultimately both are completely forgotten.

CHAPTER TWELVE

The Subconscious and Your Relationships

Partnership unites couples in love. Unity and solidarity are their destiny and their joy. But this union in itself is not a fountain of happiness. Only in awareness of the principles of life and spiritual values are two people able to give each other joy and happiness.

Even if you are alone and longing for a partner, you will experience something interesting here: the subconscious will bring two people together. So you will find your suitable partner for life by meditating on attributes and characteristics you desire in your ideal partner.

Your Subconscious Mind and Relationship Issues

Ignorance of the functions and powers of the mind is the root cause of all trouble in an intimate relationship. Friction between partners can be solved by each using the law of mind correctly. By praying together, they stay together. The contemplation of divine ideals, the study of the laws of life, the mutual agreement on a common purpose and plan, and the enjoyment of personal freedom bring about that harmonious union, that sense of oneness where the two become one.

The best time to prevent a breakup is before making a life commitment to one another. It is not wrong to try to get out of a very bad situation. But why get into the bad situation in the first place? Would it not be better to give attention to the real cause of relationship discord—in other words, to really get at the root of the matter involved?

As with all other problems between two individuals in a close relationship, breakups (and the resulting legal issues, in the case of a married couple) are directly traceable to lack of knowledge of the working and interrelationship of the conscious and subconscious mind.

The Meaning of a Committed Relationship

For a committed relationship to be real, it must be established on a spiritual foundation. It must be of the heart, and the heart is the chalice of love. Honesty, sincerity, kindness, and integrity are also forms of love. Each partner should be perfectly honest and sincere with the other. It is not a true union when someone marries for money, power, or social standing, because this indicates a lack of sincerity, honesty, and true love. Such a union is a farce, a sham, and a masquerade.

When one partner thinks, "I am tired of working; I want to get married because I want security," that premise is false. The laws of mind are being applied incorrectly. Security depends not on another person but upon one's knowledge of the interaction of the conscious and subconscious mind and its application.

You will never lack for wealth or health if you apply the techniques outlined in the respective chapters of this book. Your wealth comes to you independent of your husband, wife, father, mother, or anyone else.

Nor do you need to rely on anyone else for peace, joy, inspiration, guidance, love, security, happiness, or anything in the world. Your security and peace of mind come from your knowledge of the inner powers within you and from the constant use of the laws of your own mind in a constructive fashion. You don't need a partner for any of that.

How to Attract the Ideal Partner

You are now acquainted with the way your subconscious mind works. You know that whatever you impress upon it will be experienced in your world.

Begin now to impress your subconscious mind with the qualities and characteristics you desire in a partner.

The following is an excellent technique: Sit at night in a comfortable chair or lie down in a comfortable place, close your eyes, let go, relax the body, and become very quiet, passive, and receptive. Talk to your subconscious mind and say this:

> I am now attracting my ideal partner, who is honest, sincere, loyal, faithful, peaceful, happy, and prosperous. These qualities I admire are sinking down into my subconscious mind now. As I dwell upon these characteristics, they become a part of me and are embodied subconsciously. I know there is an irresistible law of attraction and that I attract to me my life partner according to my subconscious belief. I attract that which I feel to be true in my subconscious mind. I know I can contribute to peace and happiness. We feel mutual love, respect, and admiration. Neither of us owns or controls the other or desires to do so. Each of us is free and freely accepts our commitment to one another.

Practice this process of populating your subconscious mind with thoughts of attraction, love, devotion, and mutual respect and adoration. Then, you will have the joy of attracting to you a partner possessing the qualities and characteristics you mentally dwelled upon. Your subconscious intelligence will open up a pathway whereby both of you will meet, according to the irresistible and changeless flow of your own subconscious mind in union with that of your partner's. Have a keen desire to give the best that is in you of love, devotion, and cooperation. Be receptive to this gift of love that you have given to your subconscious mind.

No Need for a Third Mistake

Recently a teacher said to me, "I have had three husbands and all three have been passive, submissive, and dependent on me to make all decisions and govern everything. Why do I attract such types of men?"

I asked her whether she had known before their marriage that her second husband was submissive, and she replied, "Of course not. Had I known, I would not have married him."

Apparently she had not learned anything from the first mistake. The trouble was with her own personality. She was domineering, and unconsciously wanted someone submissive so that she could be in control. All this was unconscious motivation, and her subconscious picture attracted to her what she subjectively wanted. She had to learn to break the pattern by adopting the right prayer process.

How She Broke the Negative Pattern

The woman in my example learned a simple truth. What you subconsciously desire is what you attract into your life. The following is the specific prayer she used to break the old subconscious pattern and attract to her the ideal mate:

> I am building into my mentality the type of man I deeply desire. The man I attract for a husband is strong, assertive, loving, successful, honest, loyal, and faithful. He finds love and happiness with me. I know he wants me, and I want him. I am honest, sincere, loving, kind, and strong. I have wonderful gifts to offer him. They are goodwill, a joyous heart, and a healthy body. He offers me the same. It is mutual. I give and I receive. Divine intelligence knows where this man is, and the deeper wisdom of my subconscious mind is now bringing both of us together in its own way, and we recognize each other immediately. I release this request to my subconscious mind, which knows how to bring my request to pass. I give thanks for the perfect answer.

She prayed in this manner night and morning, affirming these truths and knowing that through frequent occupation of the mind she would reach the mental equivalent of what she sought.

Several months went by. She had a great number of dates and social engagements, none of which was agreeable to her. When she was about to question, waiver, doubt, and vacillate, she reminded herself that the infinite intelligence was bringing it to pass in its own way and that there was nothing to be concerned about. Her final decree in her divorce proceedings was granted, which brought her a great sense of release and mental freedom.

Shortly afterward she went to work as a receptionist in a doctor's office. She told me that the minute she saw the physician, she knew he was the man she was praying about. Apparently he knew it, too, because he proposed to her the first week she was in the office, and their subsequent marriage was ideally happy.

She got what she prayed for because she claimed it mentally until she reached the point of saturation. In other words, she mentally and emotionally united with her idea, and that idea brought her desire to fruition.

Should I Get a Divorce?

Divorce is an individual problem. It cannot be generalized. In some cases, of course, there never should have been a marriage. In some cases, divorce is not the solution, no more so than marriage is the solution for loneliness. Divorce may be right for one person and wrong for another. A divorced person may be far more sincere and noble than many who stay in a bad marriage.

If you are in doubt as to what to do, ask for guidance, knowing that there is always an answer, and you will receive it. Follow the lead that comes to you in the silence of your soul. It speaks to you in peace.

Example: I once talked with a woman whose husband was a drug addict, an ex-convict, a wife-beater, and a nonprovider. She had been told it was wrong to get a divorce. I explained to her that marriage is of the heart. If two hearts blend harmoniously, lovingly, and sincerely, that is the ideal marriage. The pure action of the heart is love.

Following this explanation she knew what to do. She knew in her heart that there is no divine law that compelled her to be browbeaten, intimidated, and beaten because someone said, "I pronounce you husband and wife."

Drifting into Divorce

Recently a young couple, married for only a few months, were seeking a divorce. I discovered that the young man had a constant fear that his wife would leave him. He expected rejection, and he believed that she would be unfaithful. These thoughts haunted his mind and became an obsession with him. His mental attitude was one of separation and suspicion. She felt unresponsive to him; it was his own feeling or atmosphere of loss and separation operating through them. This brought about a condition or action in accordance with the mental pattern behind it. There is a law of action and reaction, or cause and effect. The thought is the action, and the response of the subconscious mind is the reaction.

His wife left home and asked for a divorce, which is what he feared and believed she would do.

Divorce takes place first in the mind; the legal proceedings follow after. These two young people were full of resentment, fear, suspicion, and anger. These attitudes weaken, exhaust, and debilitate the whole being. They learned that hate divides and that love unites. They began to realize what they had been doing with their minds. Neither one of them knew the law of mental action, and they were misusing their minds and bringing on chaos and misery. These two people went back together at my suggestion and experimented with prayer therapy.

They began to radiate love, peace, and goodwill to each other. Each one practiced radiating harmony, health, peace, and love to the other, and they alternated in the reading of the Psalms every night. Their marriage is growing more beautiful every day.

The Nagging Partner

If your partner nags, it's usually either a sign that you're being passive aggressive (resisting requests) or you're not giving your partner the attention and appreciation expected. If your laziness or procrastination is at the root of the nagging, admit it, and put forth some effort in correcting your ways. If you're neglecting your partner emotionally, give your partner love and attention and express your appreciation. Praise and exalt all your partner's many good points.

Some partners nag in an attempt to mold the other into a preconceived ideal. This is about the quickest way in the world to drive someone out of your life. You do not own and you cannot control another human being. Trying to do so will leave you frustrated and the other person bitter and resentful.

Partners should give one another attention and praise each other for their constructive and wonderful qualities instead of looking for petty flaws and foibles.

The Brooding Partner

A brooding partner is usually bitter or resentful over something—career, relationship, or other circumstances. The bitterness and resentment are then turned against the partner, who is usually powerless to help, especially if the person who's doing the brooding refuses to discuss the situation. Brooding is actually a way of being unfaithful—turning one's attention to something that's negative and destructive to the relationship. If you brood, you are not being faithful to your commitment to love, cherish, and honor your partner.

If you notice that you are brooding, you must address the root of your bitterness and resentment openly with your partner's help. If it is something in the relationship, that needs to be addressed with open, honest communication. If it is outside of the relationship, your partner deserves to know about it and can perhaps help by offering a different perspective or a solution.

In some cases, you may be able to think your way out of whatever is making you bitter and resentful. Usually, it is something that is standing in the way of what you desire, in which case, you simply need to engage the power of your subconscious mind. Brooding is a negative emotion, and it will bring into your life more of what you are brooding over. You must shift to a more positive mindset and make a conscious effort to be kind, considerate, and courteous to everyone, including and especially your partner.

The Biggest Mistake

A great mistake is to discuss your relationship problems or difficulties with neighbors and relatives. Suppose, for example, a wife says to the neighbor, "John barely gets off the couch. He treats my mother abominably, drinks to excess, and is constantly abusive and insulting."

Now, this wife is degrading and belittling her husband in the eyes of all the neighbors and relatives. He no longer appears as the ideal husband to them. Never discuss your relationship problems with anyone except your partner and a trained counselor. Why cause numerous people to think negatively of your relationship or your partner? Moreover, as you discuss and dwell upon your partner's shortcomings, you are actually creating these states within yourself. Who is thinking and feeling it? You are. As you think and feel, so are you.

Relatives will usually give you the wrong advice. It is usually biased and prejudiced because it is not given in an impersonal way. Any advice you receive that violates the Golden Rule, which is a cosmic law, is not good or sound.

It is well to remember that no two human beings ever lived beneath the same roof without clashes of temperament or periods of hurts and strain. Never display the unhappy side of your relationship to your friends. Keep your quarrels to yourself. Refrain from criticism and condemnation of your partner.

Don't Try to Make Someone Who They Are Not

Never try to make someone the person you think that person should be. Attempting to change someone against that person's nature is always foolish, and many times results in a dissolution of the relationship. Criticism, coercion, and other tactics commonly used to change a person destroy the person's pride and self-esteem and arouse a spirit of contrariness and resentment that proves fatal to the relationship.

Adjustments are needed, of course, but if you have a good look inside your own mind, and study your character and behavior, you will find so many shortcomings, they will keep you busy the rest of your life. If you say, "I will make him over into what I want," you are looking for trouble and asking for misery. You will have to learn the hard way that there is no one to change but yourself.

Pray Together and Stay Together Through Steps in Prayer

The first step: Never carry over from one day to another accumulated irritations arising from little disappointments. Be sure to forgive each other for any sharpness before you retire at night. The moment you awaken in the morning, claim infinite intelligence is guiding you in all your ways. Send out loving thoughts of peace, harmony, and love to your partner, to all members of the family, and to the whole world.

The second step: Say grace at breakfast. Give thanks for the wonderful food, for your abundance, and for all your blessings. Make sure that no problems, worries, or arguments shall enter into the table conversation; the same applies at dinner time. Say to your partner, "I appreciate all you are doing, and I radiate love and goodwill to you all day long."

The third step: Partners should alternate in praying each night. Do not take your partner for granted. Show your appreciation and love. Think appreciation and goodwill, rather than condemnation, criticism, and nagging. The way to build a peaceful home and a happy union is to use a foundation of love, beauty, harmony, mutual respect, faith in God, and all things good. Read the 23rd, 27th, and 91st Psalms, the 11th chapter of Hebrews, the 13th chapter of I Corinthians, and other great texts of the Bible before going to sleep. As you practice these truths, your relationship will grow more and more blessed through the years.

Ignorance of the mental-spiritual laws is the cause of all unhappy partner relationships. Why don't you enter into a discussion with your partner about the principles as taught in this book? Maybe you would like to introduce a new ritual into your relationship: prayer. It is completely up to you which form this will take; you can be creative about it—one of the possibilities will be presented to you on the pages to come.

Exercise: Positive Prayer

In your mind, imagine your partner as happy, healthy, vibrant, reliable, kind, level-headed, and affectionate. Thank God or life for this partner and this relationship. Let these thoughts and imaginings become a habit and you will experience that your union isn't only "made in heaven" but can also be "heaven on earth."

Insight into Practice

Your relationships to other people are first and foremost determined by the feelings you have toward yourself. To be able to enter into a harmonious and productive interaction with other people, it is important that you first learn to like yourself and expect only the best from relations to others.

You can shape your relationships with other people more positively and rewardingly. No matter how your family ties, your contacts, and your friendships may look at the moment, you can lastingly improve them by using the exercises that are presented here.

For best results, record yourself reading the following exercise aloud and then play it back as you perform the exercise.

Relaxation Exercise

Lie down comfortably on your back, legs stretched out next to each other, your arms loosely beside your body. Are you really comfortable? If not, change your position until you feel truly at ease. If you have found your spot like this, take a moment to arrive. In a moment I will ask you to breathe in and out three times and to close your eyes on the third exhalation.

First, breathe in and out once. You are prepared to relax your body and your mind. Breathe in and out for the second time. When you breathe out, relax even more. Breathe in for the third time now and close your eyes when you exhale. You sink deeper and deeper and relax more and more. You are glad that you're giving yourself time to enjoy this inner tranquility. Let this moment happen and let all the images, feelings, voices, and energies simply vanish.

Feel how free and light your body feels. Listen within where you can experience and perceive in a particularly beautiful manner. And now imagine a beautiful summer landscape. You are walking across a forest meadow, the birds are chirping, close by a little brook is burbling. You approach the little brook.

You lie down next to it in the soft moss and feel how your body relaxes more and more. The flowing water carries you ever deeper into relaxation. You lie heavily and relaxed on the soft moss.

Relaxation is spreading through your whole body. Relaxation streams into your legs and feet. Now it flows into your belly. Your breathing makes your abdominal wall rise and fall. Your pelvis is very relaxed and at the same time and simultaneously all your abdominal muscles relax. You are filled by a warm, relaxing sensation. It is as if the sun shone within your belly and its warming rays scatter in your whole body. The whole trunk is completely relaxed.

Now relax your shoulder muscles. Relaxation streams into your arms and hands, the muscles in your neck and head relax. All the muscles of head and face relax. Now you see that you're sitting immediately in front of the little brook's source. The water springs forth from a mountain and you can see a very special brilliance, radiance, sparkling and glittering. The water is shining and clear. And you feel how the light of the well fills each cell of your body. And you feel happy to experience this very special feeling of the well within yourself. You are in a state of profound connectedness, at one with yourself and with life.

Now you let the rainbow-colored light of the well shine forth even more strongly and radiantly. And you feel how light courses through you and expands within you. You now are within a wonderful shroud of light. And you enjoy this marvelous feeling. And this feeling intensifies with every breath. And now imagine how your life will look if you live more and more in the light of this fountain. How the new day begins and how you enjoy it. You see how you treat yourself well, how you praise yourself.

And now you see other people with whom you interact and you feel how this intense light that surrounds you changes your relationships. You see how an intense stream of light flows between you and another person. Imagine this other person in detail: wish for him or her what you wish for yourself. And all at once you feel how precious this person is for you and how precious you are for him or her. And you realize that your relationships are filled more and more with intense qualities like happiness, fun, joy, contentment, trust, vitality, and laughter. It is fun to be alive.

You like the people in your life and the people like you. And while you're lying in the soft, warm moss at the fountain, you realize how beautiful and how important it is that you treat yourself so kindly and respectfully. You pay attention to breathing well and regularly, to allow yourself breaks and eat consciously. And you learn more and more to love yourself without condition.

Now you imagine how you are surrounded by the light of the fountain while you're working. It is a very special radiance that comes from within and lends you an aura of calmness, self-confidence, success and vitality. The feeling of being successful makes contact with your colleagues and coworkers a pleasure. You realize how nice it is to support each other and to be happy together. And you are aware of the good in everything and praise it. It is easy for you to utter praise and admiration.

It is also easy for you to confidently and securely state and carry through your opinion. You are aware of yourself. You are cordial, upright, and kind. You are lively and merry. You like to give but just as much you like to receive. You deserve to experience happiness and fun in life. With every day, you are becoming more aware of your relationships with others. It is easy for you to make friends. You respect these friendships. You are able to express your feelings toward other people. You find something good in every person. It makes you happy to be in contact with other people, to support and nurture others.

You like yourself without condition. You find joy in fulfilling human relationships. People feel attracted to you and enjoy being close to you. It is also easy for you to confidently and securely state and carry through your opinion. You are aware of yourself. You are cordial, upright, and kind. You are lively and merry. You like to give but just as much you like it to receive. You deserve to experience happiness and fun in life.

With every day you are becoming more aware of your relationships with others. It is easy for you to make friends. You respect these friendships. You are able to express your feelings toward other people. You find something good in every person. It makes you happy to be in contact with other people, to support and nurture others. You like yourself without condition. You find joy in fulfilling human relationships. People feel attracted to you and enjoy being close to you.

Now the images start to slowly retract, the colors fade. Slowly you return to this room. You are growing more and more alert. You feel light, free, and gloriously rested. You are growing ever more awake. You feel light, so very light and slowly open your eyes.

The Subliminal Affirmations

All of this subliminal information will flow into your subconscious while you are reading or listening. In this way you can make the best use of the power of your subconscious. The following affirmations will strengthen your ability to have harmonious relationships:

- I love myself without condition.
- I am aware of myself.
- I am cordial, upright, and kind.

- I like to give but I also like to receive.
- I wish unto others what I wish unto myself.
- I deserve to experience lots of joy and fun in my life.
- Each day I am more aware of my relationship to others.
- It is easy for me to make friends.
- I respect these friendships.
- I am able to express my feelings toward others.
- I find something good in every person.
- I enjoy being in exchange with others, nurturing them and supporting them.
- I am able to confidently state and carry through my opinion.
- I like myself without condition.

ABOUT THE AUTHOR

A native of Ireland who resettled in the United States, Joseph Murphy (1898–1981) was a prolific and widely admired New Thought minister and writer, best known for his metaphysical classic, *The Power of Your Subconscious Mind*, an international bestseller since it first appeared on the self-help scene in 1963.

A popular speaker, Dr. Murphy lectured on both American coasts and in Europe, Asia, and South Africa as Minister-Director of the Church of Divine Science in Los Angeles. He received his PhD in psychology. His lectures and sermons were attended by thousands of people every Sunday. Millions of people tuned in to hear his daily radio program and have read the over thirty books that he has written.

His many books and pamphlets on the autosuggestive and metaphysical faculties of the human mind have entered multiple editions. Dr. Murphy is considered one of the pioneering voices of affirmative-thinking philosophy.

He has been acclaimed as a major figure in the human potential movement, the spiritual heir to writers such as James Allen, Dale Carnegie, Napoleon Hill, and Norman Vincent Peale and a precursor and inspirer of contemporary motivational writers and speakers such as Tony Robbins, Zig Ziglar, Louise Hay, and Earl Nightingale.

CPSIA information can be obtained
at www.ICGtesting.com
Printed in the USA
LVHW050204220722
723560LV00005B/16